IF THE TRUTH BE TOLD

SONAM'S STORY OF NARCISSISTIC PARENTAL ABUSE IN A SOUTH ASIAN HOUSEHOLD, AND HOW BREAKING FREE LED HER TO FIND FREEDOM.

SONAM DAVE

© 2025 Sonam Dave

All rights reserved. No portion of this book, including the illustrations, may be reproduced, stored in a retrieval system, or transmitted in any form or by any means electronic, mechanical, photocopy, recording, scanning, or other (except for brief quotations in reviews or articles without prior written permission by the publisher or author).

Disclaimer:

This book is a work of non-fiction, based on the author's personal memories, experiences, and interpretations. Some names, locations, and identifying details have been changed or omitted to protect the privacy of individuals. While every effort has been made to present events truthfully, the author and publisher do not accept responsibility for differing interpretations, omissions, or any consequences arising from the content.

This book may reference sexual violence, trauma, and abuse that may be distressing to some readers. These details are shared for the purpose of healing, awareness, and advocacy, not to sensationalise or harm. All content is the sole responsibility of the author and reflects their lived experience.

The views expressed are those of the author and do not necessarily represent those of the publisher.

Published by Powerful Books.

ISBN 978-1-83522-059-7 (eBook)

ISBN 978-1-83522-061-0 (HC)

ISBN 978-1-83522-060-3 (PB)

CONTENTS

Preface — vii

Terminology Guide — 1
1. The Real Conversation — 5
2. Coward — 27
3. Liar — 39
4. Symbolic — 50
5. Celebrations — 60
6. I'm only on this earth to help — 69
7. Empty Threats — 74
8. Comparison — 78
9. The things we tell ourselves — 84
10. Am I a Narcissist? — 93
11. Extended family alienation — 97
12. Believe people when they show you who they are, the first time — 101
13. The Other Sibling — 106
14. Survivor — 111
15. A note to the South Asian Community — 121
16. Spiritual calling — 127
17. Did I ever like them? — 130
18. Life after trauma — 132
19. For you — 135

About the Author — 141

*Thank you to the people who supported my love of books, reading and writing from a young age.
Thank you to my loved ones who supported me throughout, and are my pillars of strength.
Lastly, thank you to the Powerful Books community for providing me not only an opportunity to be heard, seen, and understood, but also connecting me with other survivors who I'll never forget.*

PREFACE

Everything wrong happens in Mum's house.
Everything cruel happens in Mum's house.
This house is not safe or secure; if anything,
*   this house is full of fear and isolation.*
The house is a trap, with tricks and scams
*   around every corner.*
Your only solace is your room, which has
*   four plastered walls that act as a thin*
*   barrier while the toxicity seeps through.*
A temporary escape.
In Mum's house, it's all her rules, all her
*   conditions, and only her way.*
Mum will sit high and mighty in her house
*   at the top of her manmade throne, only to*
*   control and manipulate all those at the*
*   bottom.*
I was one of those at the bottom for most of
*   my life. Clawing my way through the*
*   trauma and the pain, always keeping a*
*   low profile to ensure that I don't get into*

the firing line, but she will always be watching from the high tower, preparing to start the first battle in the never-ending war.

Always falling... never flying.

Always afraid and never evolving.

Mum's house will make you question who you are.

Mum's house will want to keep you where you are.

These are only half of the things that happen in Mum's house.

In Mum's house, Dad is non-existent to the human eye, but he is like the dark shadow that supports his evil wife, and will sacrifice himself just so she is satisfied. The black shadow will always move without purpose, but will reveal his true ways under her commands.

The dark shadow that lives in Mum's house will engulf you in his darkness and torment when he feels like it's time for him to take over. The dark shadow only gets attention when she enjoys the view.

In Mum's house, she feeds off the pain you carry, she feeds off the burden you hold, and she feeds off the anger you store.

No one is safe in Mum's house, that's why you GET OUT.

Run as fast as you can, as quick as your feet will allow and your body to hold, run and don't look back. Don't ever look

> *back. If you do, then you will be trapped there forever and a day.*

Before I share my story with you, the fact that I've even written and published a book blows my mind, as one core memory of being a young girl was my love for reading and one day dreaming of becoming an author.

I was sat in the living room, on the big comfy chair in the corner where there was the painting of the two people dancing above me, it looked like they were participating in some type of 'flamenco' dance. I had the chair adjusted so that I had the right amount of natural light shining through on the pages of the book I was reading, by the author Lemony Snicket. I love reading under natural light. I'm truly enjoying myself and letting my imagination run wild as I read intensely, and in she walks... my mum.

She sits down on her own chair on the other side of the big living room that we had, and begins to check her mobile phone. I thought we'd be sharing a peaceful, co-existing moment — but no. Soon after, my mum looks up from her phone, disgust in her eyes, and asks what I'm doing. I explained I was reading, and she said, 'You need to stop reading those books here. I am going to be on the phone now, so it's best you get out of my sight. ' That was one of the first times I felt that my love for books couldn't be shared with anyone, as it wouldn't be celebrated. So I didn't mention my love for books to many people for years after that.

TERMINOLOGY GUIDE

Narcissist - Narcissistic personality disorder is a mental health condition in which people have an unreasonably high sense of their own importance. They need and seek too much attention and want people to admire them. People with this disorder may lack the ability to understand or care about the feelings of others.

Manipulation - The action of influencing someone in a clever or unscrupulous way.

Emotional Abuse - Emotional abuse is any type of abuse that involves the continual emotional mistreatment of a child. It's sometimes called psychological abuse. Emotional abuse can involve deliberately trying to scare, humiliate, isolate or ignore a child.

Enabler - A person who encourages or enables negative or self-destructive behaviour in another.

Golden Child - In a family dynamic, a *golden child* is a child who is favoured or perceived as perfect. Often expected to excel in everything and be held to a higher standard than their siblings. This can create an imbalance in the family, potentially leading to resentment or feelings of inadequacy among other children.

Scapegoat - A person who is blamed for the wrongdoings, mistakes, or faults of others, especially for reasons of expediency.

Lost Child - No official definition. More of an expression of oneself, feeling lost as a child. Not being seen or heard by respected caregivers.

Emotional Blackmail - Emotional blackmail refers to manipulating someone through guilt, threats, or other emotional tactics to get them to comply with the blackmailer's wishes. It's a form of control where the blackmailer uses someone's vulnerability or sense of obligation to exert their will.

Abuse - To treat someone with cruelty or violence, especially regularly or repeatedly.

Narcissistic Rage - Narcissistic rage is an intense emotional outburst, often characterised by aggression or passive-aggression, that can occur when a narcissist feels their self-esteem or grandiose sense of self is threatened.

Trauma - A deeply distressing or disturbing experience.

No Contact - No contact refers to intentionally cutting off all communication with a person. This includes phone calls, texts, social media interactions, and even in-person encounters. The purpose is often to help the individual heal, process emotions, and move forward.

Neglect - Fail to care for properly.

Abandonment - The action or fact of abandoning or being abandoned.

Smear Campaign - A smear campaign is an intentional, premeditated effort to undermine an individual's or group's reputation, credibility, and character.

Flying Monkey - In the context of psychology, particularly related to narcissistic abuse, *flying monkeys* refer to people who are enlisted by a narcissist to do their bidding or spread their narrative, often by attacking or manipulating others on their behalf. They are essentially extensions of the narcissist's control, acting as enablers and pawns in their manipulative schemes.

Triangulation - The use of threats of exclusion or manipulation to divide and conquer a situation.

Walking On Eggshells - To be very careful about what you say or do to someone because they may be easily upset or offended.

Gaslight - Manipulating someone using psychological methods into questioning their own sanity or powers of reasoning.

Family Alienation - Family alienation refers to a situation where one parent or guardian actively undermines a child's relationship with the other parent or guardian or family member, often through manipulation, coercion, or negative communication. This can lead to the child rejecting or becoming hostile towards the other parent or family member without a legitimate reason.

Boundaries - Boundaries are personal limits that individuals set for themselves to protect their own well-being, values, and sense of self within a relationship. They define what a person is comfortable with and what they will not tolerate.

PTSD - The short term for post-traumatic stress disorder is a condition of persistent emotional and mental stress occurring as a result of an injury or severe psychological shock. Typically, it may involve the disturbance of sleep and constant vivid recall of the experience, with dulled responses to others and the outside world.

Hypervigilance - Hypervigilance is a condition in which the nervous system is inaccurately filtering sensory information, and the individual is in an enhanced state of sensory sensitivity. This appears to be linked to a dysregulated nervous system, which can often be caused by traumatic events or complex PTSD.

Freedom - This is my own definition, which is being free of anyone's opinions, expectations, choices, and criticism. This type of freedom cannot be bought, but instead should be the most valued for the soul.

1

THE REAL CONVERSATION

My personal account of my story is not told in a strict chronological order, and that's because narcissistic abuse doesn't happen in that same order. The abuse clouds your judgment, confuses the fuck out of you, and makes you overthink and question everything. The reason I've decided to share my story this way is to touch upon the importance of how this psychological abuse works, almost taking the reader on a mental journey of this experience and the memories it leaves you with. I'll be jumping back and forth — from childhood memories of where it all began, to the realisations that came years later, and everything in between — leading up to going no contact, and finally, life after my trauma. This story contains live updates too, from what happened to me while I was in the process of writing.

So let's start with memories as a child. The positive ones people might remember may be eating ice-creams in the heat of summer, or feeling that mixture of anxiousness and adrenaline on their first day of school. Memories can last a lifetime, and there's always a starting point, but when you are in an environment of abuse, the memories can get hazy and confusing. The only aspect you remember is the depth of your feelings, which are always of sadness, grief and pain. Therefore, I wanted to start my story by sitting you in the middle of the mind of someone who has suffered this abuse and is now unpacking years of trauma, using publishing as a tool for the process.

When asked by my therapist, "What is your earliest childhood memory?" I try to swallow even though my throat is dead dry. I pause, part my lips as if I'm about to speak, but then I don't. My therapist didn't get to know in that first session what my earliest childhood memory was, but what he didn't hear that evening I heard loudly in my mind.

America, aged 9, hair covered in head lice with the mother and babies — I'm uncomfortable, but still happy. This statement will seem shocking to most, but this was my reality. We had gone on one of my mum's ego-filled holidays to America to visit my uncle (who, I later disturbingly found out participated in a smear campaign against me and my sister, and I believe holds his own narcissist traits). On the holiday, everything was great, Mum was acting happy, and Dad seemed calm. My brother and I would hang out with my two cousins, and on the surface, it seemed fine. But why was I always wearing my hair in pigtails?

Itch Itch Itch.

Now we're off to the Mall of America, and it's the first time I've seen rides inside a shopping centre, whizzing past families, happiness, and ice cream. My mum would be straight to the clothes shops, searching for bargains and buying clothes that never truly satisfied her, she just loved an excuse to buy shit. Skip to that evening, to me scratching my head in the basement bathroom, tears streaming down my face. I felt so ashamed that I had tiny creatures running riot in my hair, adult-sized head lice falling into the sink when I shook my head. But no one knew, or that's what I convinced myself of as I felt such shame, this is a me problem and no one else's. But someone did know, my mum knew all along. She knew the minute we stepped on that fucking plane. I carried this burden just before we celebrated my 10th birthday in America. Weeks of wearing my hair up, or at one point, I started sporting a cap. "How cute she's copying her brother", said a family member. No, it wasn't cute at all; the cap represented my shame and neglect.

Finally, she gave in and began looking through my hair, but let's be honest, she wasn't looking to solve the problem; instead, she wanted to hide it. Evenings went by, and she'd take me into the basement bathroom and squash the head lice herself with her unruly, long nails... *squish, crack, repeat*. I stared blankly into the mirror and numbed my pain.

Do I even remember when the issue got resolved? Honestly, I don't. Children get head lice from schools, siblings, cousins, whatever it might be, and it doesn't mean you are dirty, as they used to *tease* you at school. But what was unacceptable was a parent keeping you that way. While she bought her Coach handbags from TJ Maxx, she couldn't spend ten dollars on a saline solution for my head. Unfortunately, because my head lice were never taken seriously or treated immediately, the head lice would go, and then I found myself a few months later catching and having them again.

A few years later, I turned 16, and I was finally rid of the head lice for good, but I remember the emotions I felt around my own hair. It didn't feel pretty or nice, it felt dirty and discarded. I only really knew one or two hairstyles, and they were always meant to cover up the issue. I don't ever remember my mum lovingly brushing my hair. I just knew the feeling of her frustrated fingers having to search my hair quickly to get rid of the issue, the easiest way she could. She would hurry me over, sit me down, and go through my hair. I could tell from her energy that she was fed up and couldn't care less about helping me. She never asked how this was affecting me, or if she was being a bit too rough with my scalp, which she always was.

I promised myself after turning 16 that I'd never let her touch my hair again.

I've only come to discover in my adult years that people who don't really remember their childhood may have experienced abuse. This rings true for me, as I don't have a strong recollection of a happy childhood; it just seems to feel numb, and my mind goes blank. I hear so many people recall the wonderful memories of playing, having fun and experiencing what it was like to be a child. They can call out certain locations they went on holiday, foods that they tasted for the first time and the friends they made along the way. They especially would remember the fond memories with a parent or family member that felt like love, or a time they bonded over an activity. I'd always listen to the stories that people would share and be happy for them, knowing deep down I don't have any of my own. When I reflect back, the only things I remember are the behaviours of my parents — watching them not necessarily be happy, as there was always something to complain, moan and whinge about, or something bad that was happening. I remember hearing all of my parents' troubles, whether it was to do with their health, their marriage or finances. I don't recall any one-to-one moments with my parents where they'd interact with me, take me out or read a story to me. I don't have any memories of going to the park or the cinema with my parents. We never went out for family meals to a restaurant, and never went to any adventure soft plays.

See, my mum was very calculated and she would only participate in things that benefited her. I do remember she had a job when we lived in London as a child minder. That woman, as a child minder, makes me truly feel sick when I think of it now. From what I know, she never outwardly abused the kids she looked after, but what she did instead was make us all interact and play together. She would then slowly step back from her responsibilities, as I was slightly older than the kids she would look after, so she'd get me to lead the way and play with the children. She would even get me to go upstairs when they'd go down for their afternoon nap and wake them up, and bring them downstairs so they could be fed. This was when I realised I liked helping people, because I'd always get some sort of emotional reward back, a smile, hug or thank you, and my day would be made. But the tough reality is that a young child shouldn't be helping her mum do her job.

That's why my memories of being a child were pretty bleak, and often involved escaping and using a lot of imaginative play to pass my time if I wasn't at school. If you ask me about any memories from around the ages of 6 or before, I'd tell you I just don't know if I have any.

The household knew no form of communication, unless it was verbally abusive. I got used to either being silent or running the risk of causing an argument if I spoke my mind. My mum would provide the bare minimum communication if it was needed, and my dad, well, he may as well have been mute, as his vocabulary only consisted of three words: "Are you okay?" But let me make this clear, his three words weren't ever out of concern, they were just to fill the gap. So if my answer was "Yes", then it would be a closed conversation; he wouldn't need to dig any further to ask any details. Since I was a little girl, I could never explain my true feelings to my dad as he never created an emotionally safe space for me to do so. Therefore, without trust, people are not able to fully be vulnerable with their loved ones, are they? One of the reasons he wasn't an emotionally safe person was because he would let his wife win in every single argument or threatening moment. He would succumb to her and would never defend or protect me when I needed him. I knew that he was my mum's slave, slave to the twisted games she would play, and no matter how hard I tried, there was no getting through to my dad. To this day, he stays by her side. Whether some may see him as a victim who couldn't free himself, I will always see him as a failure. Not even just for me, but for his own life.

The conversation that lasted a lifetime. I always knew I loved my sister, like truly loved and cared about her, since I was young. If my therapist were a little more specific and asked about a childhood memory involving my sister, I'd have told him this one.

I was sitting on the big black beanie cushion in her warm living room. I'm watching a *FRIENDS* boxset on the TV and eating something sugary — my brother-in-law was always so generous with his food. I'm smiling, laughing even, and not having a care in the world because I knew that at my sister's house, it felt like home. Each time I was at hers, I experienced a fraction of love. So in my head, I had internalised, home means pain and sister's house means love.

This became extremely confusing during my adolescent years.

My sister decided to speak to me. This wasn't a general conversation, but a serious conversation with a heavy tone. She told me that I needed to be careful at home around our mum. She explained that now I was hitting a certain age, nearer to 13, it would start the same way it did for her. She told me to be strong and that one day it would get better — that I'd be able to leave, that there was a way out... that day didn't come until I was nearly 30 years old. She told me that I could speak to her, but I knew from her expression of concern that she wanted me to be safe, and she was deeply hurt that she would witness the cycle of abuse. In my mind, everything I'd always known changed; the bubble had burst because even though I knew my mum wasn't right, she was still my mum. I told my sister that I loved her, but that I loved Mum too. She said that was fine — and that, in time, I'd figure it out on my own. And I did. I trailed back to Dad's car with my pink Tinkerbell suitcase, feeling a deep sadness about leaving my sister's house. This sadness would stay with me always, each time I'd have to hug her goodbye and say bye to the rest of her family. I always felt like the odd one out, because as soon as I stepped into Dad's car, there was a robotic voice to ask if I was okay — no enthusiasm to talk to his daughter, no interest in asking what I'd been up to.

We would then carry on in bleak silence back to Mum's house.

The acting would begin the minute I walked through that door: "Did you enjoy your sister's house? How is everyone? What did you eat? Where did you go?" Usually, I would succumb and answer all her questions and give everything away about how much I loved it at my sisters. I didn't realise she would use this information against me in the future. But this time, I looked at her differently. I studied her face and watched her mouth curl up evilly, her eyes black with no emotion. I could sense in her voice that she wasn't enthusiastic about me being back home either, but rather, she wanted intel on my sister's house. This time, I just gave a vague answer and said, "It was just fine, but I am tired and want to go to my room", so she let me go. As I unpacked my bags — one of the countless times I'd pack and unpack for the rest of my life — I felt I couldn't trust her anymore after the conversation my sister had with me. As time went on, I realised I couldn't trust her because of everything my sister said, and as much as I wished it wouldn't come true, it did. The promises my mum made to me always turned out to be false. There was definitely something not right with Mum.

The relationship my mum had with my sister was very strange. One minute I'd hear them talking over the phone, the next they'd be arguing, and I mean full-on shouting and raging on the phone. I always wondered what caused this erratic change in emotion from them both. I started realising as I got older and when I was forming a bond with my sister, that our mum was obsessed with her. I mean, truly obsessed. Now, when I say this, I don't mean that passionate type of obsession like she was the favourite child, I mean she was obsessed with hating my sister, truly hating on her for just existing. The conversations I'd have with my mum from a young age would always involve my sister. My mum would either be bitching about her, or asking me if I can find out information about what goes on in their household. Riddle me wrong, but if someone hates someone, why would they want to know every detail about them? This didn't apply to my mum, as she loved talking shit about my sister and her life. This is when I stepped into the role of the invisible child. I wasn't the hot topic of debate like my sister was, and I wasn't the favourite like my brother was. On reflection, this was probably one of the safer options, as I would only receive collateral damage the majority of the time as a child. So what happens to the invisible child? Let me give you the perspective.

POV from the invisible child

Here I am, but nobody sees me, hears me or cares for me. I walk alone through the house, witnessing a lot of abuse. My parents are talking badly about my sister, mocking her and laughing behind her back. I internalise these feelings as I carry the emotion of my sister's pain, whilst she's not even here. I look to my brother, who just decides to ignore the comments about our older sister and hides himself away in his room, where he's got all he ever wanted: PlayStation, PC, and his music player. What he's really thinking, nobody knows. I didn't know my place in that family, I couldn't figure out what my role was because it seemed that everyone had a role but me. So I would try and make myself seen, I would try and have nice conversations with my parents, but

> *that never lasted long as my mum would rather speak to her friends than me. My dad's body language gave off more than his speech; the way he barely made eye contact with me whilst I would speak to him meant he was not interested. There we go — reminded of my place again. Invisible child. You're only seen when the parent needs you. You're only seen if you offer some type of service to them. So, back up the staircase I go, I shut my bedroom door and stare out of the window, one day I will be seen and one day I will get to live. I just had no idea when that day would come.*

Money was always a strange topic in Mum's house. One minute we had it, and I mean lots of it, to the point where she'd be booking the next trip out to the States. Not just visiting Minnesota, but California, Florida, and even Vegas. The next minute, we had no money, which meant she didn't have enough money to buy me a new pair of jeans from H&M or get my hair cut at a hairdresser of my choosing. So you can imagine how confusing that would have been for a pre-teen. Those pre-teen years were mentally scarring. Mum had realised that I would be old enough soon to make money, and she conditioned my brain to feel sorry for her because she couldn't work, saying, "After I gave birth to you, you gave me rheumatoid arthritis, so you're the reason for me being this way". When you have this ingrained in your head your whole life, it makes you feel guilty. I thought, *We don't seem to have enough money — so how can I make more and not just help myself, but the family too?*

Here comes me working at 15 years old at music festivals, serving Chinese fast food behind a tent counter. Now, don't get me wrong, these were my best summers. I was unchained from Mum's house and was able to be free and discover what being a teen is about. My love of music was amplified by seeing certain artists live, feeling the music course through my veins, and resonating with the deep, raw emotion certain lyrics brought out in me. I was surrounded by all my closest friends, as we all volunteered to work together all summer. We were taken away in a minibus to different parts of the UK to work, and returned with a big brown envelope full of hard-earned cash. Once more, I'd dread going back to Mum's house. This sad feeling was so deeply rooted in my soul that I'd feel it every single time I came back from anywhere that brought me joy. So when I discovered at the age of 29 that I could live on my own terms in my place, it was a very cathartic part of my journey.

On the minibus ride back to dropping everyone off home, everyone would share how exhausted they were and that they couldn't wait to sleep in their beds and not a tent or caravan. These things were common ground for me too; what wasn't common ground was the fact that everyone would speak about what their mum would make for them for dinner, a nice hearty home-cooked meal, something that I rarely experienced. I'd have to mask in front of my friends that I, too, couldn't wait to have dinner when I got home, but that was the furthest away from the truth.

The front door would open, and there she was, strategically placed in her chair in her house, plotting and planning in her disturbed mind how she was going to snatch this money from me. If you research a narcissist and money, it will highlight the immense obsession they have with it, they'd kill for it. As she waits, I make sure my brown envelope is nowhere to be seen, tucked away in my backpack. Now I know how this conversation is going to go, as it'll start off sweet, then she'll spit evil from her mouth. After she did her polite check to see if I was okay, she put a hot water bottle in my bed so it would be toasty when I went to sleep. She hadn't made any dinner, but said she'd make whatever I wanted later on. The attention rapidly turned to how much I got paid and where the money is. Just to bring some context, this is a 50-something-year-old woman asking her youngest daughter at the mere age of 15 for half her pay packet.

I'd begun to slowly have a voice, I refused to give the money, and before I knew it, she went into her narcissistic fit of rage, or as they call it, full-blown rage. The pitch her voice could reach was disturbing — she sounded possessed, screaming that I was a *prostitute* and didn't deserve the money. She raged about all that she did for me, about how I couldn't pay her, and how dare I question her, who did I think I was, and so much more. As a young person, you stand there in shock, your face burning as tears stream down your cheeks — your mum has just called you a prostitute, and you're still a virgin. The next thing I know, Dad walks in the room claiming he's heard the whole conversation, and he backs Mum 100%. To add, he has worn a hearing aid from before I was born and normally can't hear a thing, but when Mum shouts the house down, I'm surprised the whole street doesn't hear. I tried to explain to him that I just wanted to keep the money I made because I worked extremely hard for it, and I needed it to buy basic things that all teenagers needed, but the more I spoke, the more she would shout, and he would become abusive. I was cornered and couldn't do a damn thing but take the emotional abuse... and behold there was never a warm dinner made for me that day or any other days I'd returned home from working. This pattern repeated itself the whole summer that I worked.

The repeated pattern of abuse around money continued. My perception of a normal family would be that they buy each other presents around their birthdays and Christmas's etc. My mum would not have any of that; she would not like to accept presents being given to her by her family, as her exact words were "I'd have preferred the money, why didn't you give me the money?" This would be said the minute you'd hand over the present to her, they could be either flowers, chocolates, candles, clothes, accessories, you name it. Most mums of that generation would appreciate that their child even thought about them enough to give them a present. My mum's obsession with money also led her to take her own children's money. One year, she handed me a birthday card (I barely received presents on my birthday) and inside was £40.00. I thanked my parents and said I was heading out for the day. My mum stopped me and looked me dead in the eyes and said that the rent money was due, so I essentially needed to hand that cash back to her. I stopped in my tracks and felt disgusted with her behaviour and desperation for money. I told her how dare she ask for rent money, and for this 'birthday' money to be part of the rent money. I told her she can keep the money, as you don't give someone a gift and then expect something back in return. I felt extremely upset and violated because of this conversation. I was in my mid-late 20s at this time, I'd been making my own money and had been pretty self-sufficient from a young age, so the birthday card they both gave me seemed to be more for the sake of it anyways. She took the money and started having a go at me, saying that I was *too sensitive* and that I was taking things the wrong way. She saw my eyes swell up with tears, which always enraged her more, so they both continued to shout that they were *pensioners* and needed the money more than I did and that I was being *selfish* to not think of them, on my own birthday.

I left the house in a state, sat in my car and drove off and called my sister from an Asda parking lot, crying my eyes out. Yet again, I am still being reminded as an adult that my mum has never had any love or respect for me.

Fast forward to being in my late 20s, and my mum explicitly tells me that my name is removed from their will. My first thought was how the hell I was even in there in the first place, as she never loved me to begin with! My second thought was that I never expected money, and this was dirty money now. The only chance I'd have that money would be if it were legally binding.

A place to live holds such importance in a person's life. It provides necessities like shelter, comfort, safety, and the ability to relax. However, in this house, it wasn't that way. I only ever experienced abuse as this was Mum's playground to do whatever she pleased with whomever she pleased.

Avril Lavigne - Nobody's Home

This incident I like to call Omelette

I was around 16 years old at the time, it was a Sunday morning, and things seemed okay in the house. When I say okay, I'd refer to the sun shining through the window. I'd woken up in a good mood and was reflecting back on the happy memories from seeing my friends the day before. There was no shouting in the early hours of the morning from Mum, so I'd class this as an okay day. However, this was about to change quite quickly. Dad had made an omelette with toast and offered me a plate, and I was happy to say yes to him. However, even though Mum would make out she was the strictest vegetarian alive — because it goes against our religion to eat any form of meat — she had married a man who did eat meat in his younger days, so she was always fighting this topic. Once again, I feel her thoughts around being vegetarian were more for her image, rather than her beliefs. Out of the blue, she offered to make me scrambled eggs, as she said Dad had done too much running around that morning, indirectly telling me that I was not worthy of his efforts to feed me. I made a joke, as most teens do, that I preferred his version of cooking eggs — and that was the trigger. She completely set off in a fit of rage, saying I'm ungrateful and asking what's wrong with her cooking. I explained that I was joking and that I could make the food myself if it was such a problem. She told me to get the hell out of the kitchen and that I couldn't eat right now. I ran back upstairs, utterly frustrated as I knew this morning was too good to be true and that she was just waiting to orchestrate another emotional outburst of hers. I could hear the screaming from downstairs of her yet again calling me a prostitute, she was screaming at Dad as if he should be backing her and shouting at me, but sometimes he stayed silent. His silence would not be protection, it would be enabling. He should have damn right been shouting, but to protect me, his daughter instead, and stand up against the woman he married, to call her out on her disgusting behaviour, but no he chose to only protect himself. This clear act of selfishness meant that I never understood men, I couldn't figure them out and I later discovered in my adult life that I had a very fucked up perception of what love is because of him.

"You can't keep loving someone so that they'll love you back". This statement sums up perfectly how I navigated my way through some of my past romantic relationships. I gave too much too soon, and that wasn't necessarily because I did love the person; it was more because I was trying so hard to be loved.

Now, as the reader, you must be questioning — where is my other sibling in this - my brother? He was right there all along, witnessing all the damage that was being caused to me and the family, but he stayed silent for a long time. This mimicking of his dad represented his character in adulthood, and he decided to remain the *golden child* - the family member in the narcissistic abuse system that doesn't see or accept that there is a fundamental issue with the abuse. The golden child would not get anywhere near the level of abuse that my sister and I had. It's proven that narcissistic mums will favour their sons over their daughters because they are a non-competitive extension of themselves. This was rightly true with my brother; he never spoke back and was always very quiet, not out of being shy, but because he was protecting himself. He always made sure he was first in line to receive anything, whether that be food, money, praise or protection.

I, however, am the *invisible child*, the one who gets abandoned from the age of 7 and is left essentially to fend for herself. They weren't interested in caring for me — they just hoped someone would be ready to take on looking after me, whether it was for a long or brief time. For a very long period of my life, I felt like a burden. The weight of Sonam was heavy, and it felt a lot to handle. They had instilled in my head that I was never enough to be wanted. I remember a moment when I was crying my eyes out in a cornfield with an ex-boyfriend, adamantly telling him that I didn't want to live anymore, as no one cared about me. Suicidal ideation stuck with me for a long time.

The problem was that I didn't care about myself. I didn't pour the love into myself that had been so harshly absent in my life. I didn't give myself a chance to soar, fly and fall. It was always a case of survival, numbing out the sensitivity I've always had as a child, breaking down my emotions so they were just shattered pieces on the ground. If I were able to put that love back into myself, it would have saved me from ruining a whole heap of relationships in my life. It would also be a protector for when relationships did end, and reassure me that it wouldn't matter either way, as I knew I'd have myself, and that's all I needed. However, this need to always be fulfilled and complete came from the shambles of the childhood I'd experienced.

What I like to call this chapter is the trick of faking an illness. Now, for as long as I can remember, I have never seen my mum go to work. I've never heard her alarm clock in the morning go off, I've never heard her rushing down the stairs trying to find her shoes or making lunch for her day at work. Now this is odd, right? Everyone at school would share their stories of their parents going to work, but in reality, my parents never did. Heck, I didn't even see my dad go to work. Instead, they worked up until they lived in London, and then when we moved to Leicester, which is where most of my childhood was. They played the system, and claimed benefits left, right and centre. My mum was great at using the system to her advantage — not being able to work due to her illness and claiming benefits, and making my dad the sole carer so he'd get paid a carer's allowance. So whilst I worked from the age of 15, they sat on their arses.

Please note that some words are translated from Gujarati to English for this text.

"Hi Mum, how are you? How was your day?"

"It's ok, I've been in pain all day".

"Ok... did you need anything?"

"No, no one understands the suffering I have to go through, none of you even care!"

I panicked. "Well Mum, I'm sorry I can't do anything to change your pain, please just stay strong; we are here for you".

"Get lost, you idiot, nobody cares about me!"

Now you can only imagine, as a year 8 school girl, the mixed emotions that I'd be feeling when I came home from school. I'd try my best not to come home if I'm honest. I'd take the longer walk home, stop at the shops as my friends got sweets, or sometimes I'd be lucky enough to be invited to my best friend's house for dinner.

On the days that I couldn't do any of the above, I'd be coming home to a very emotionally unstable home, constantly walking on eggshells. I'd physically feel the energy shift, and it would be depressing. My mum struggled with rheumatoid arthritis, and every chance she would get, she'd mention it. See how I'm trying to help as a child of only 13 years old — but I'd get backlash for even trying.

This is the narcissist's way of holding power and enjoying the torment they give someone when they feel that person is responsible for their feelings. I'd hurry upstairs to my room feeling deflated, no one asks about my day... ever.

These days happened frequently, when she was in this boy-cried-wolf mentality. The rheumatoid arthritis affected her hands quite badly, so how is she conversing and laughing on the phone to her friends for hours on end? Dad just stood by and let this happen as he thought this was making her feel better, all the while we would be stalking the kitchen cupboards looking for food, as she would try to avoid making dinner for us. If I did find something to eat, it was usually expired.

The most fucked up thing about all of this, is my perception of being *ill* changed. I felt I could never be ill because who would then look after Mum? In my mind at the time, her illness was way worse than anyone else's at home, so even if I did feel unwell, I'd not get looked after, so what was the point of vocalising it? Suffer the pain in silence.

One day, we went away with some family friends from Bristol. I'd slept in the spare room, and all of a sudden, I started getting a high temperature and immediately felt ill. My friend's mum was so caring, she could hear me squirming in the middle of the night and came to help me. She got me a cool flannel for my head and sat with me. My mum, well, she didn't bother.

The illness trick got worse the older we got, because by this point, I had internalised her feelings and began seeing more of the real world and felt confused about how ill my mum really was. Many times I'd sit with her and try and get her to explain her symptoms, what the latest doctor letter said or when her next GP appointment was but I was faced with "You don't need to know any of that, not right now just listen and hear about me and how I am feeling". This made me doubt a lot of her attempts to feel better because I truly believed she enjoyed being in the pain she was in. She wanted a crutch, something she could use to manipulate against the family at any given minute to get exactly what she wanted and how she wanted it.

You might think this is crazy, someone staying ill for gain, but look it up, it's called *Munchausen syndrome*. Many people across the world do this, and no, it's not acceptable before anyone tries to rationalise this type of behaviour. It takes away the true essence of someone who is struggling with a condition, illness, or disability. But have you noticed that people who have a severe disability or condition always tend to be the most positive and resilient? I can list the illnesses my mum suffered from, because each year a new one formed. Arthritis was her main one, high blood pressure, diabetes, high cholesterol, chest pains, headaches, back pains, stomach issues, and a few other unknown problems. Let's not forget about the 3 hip replacements she's had, and a couple of falls along the way. You might be wondering why I feel the need to list all of these problems that she had — it's because she's used each and every one against me, as an excuse to cause tantrums in the family home. For a woman who suffers from these problems, she sure didn't help herself. She would catastrophise each problem she had and spend days in a chaotic state. The complaining, moaning, and crying — like she was being attacked — was the worst to deal with, because no matter how you'd try and console her, she just didn't want the support. She didn't want certain medications, but then she expected her youngest daughter to take the responsibility, not even of her illness, but more for her emotional state.

When I was young, I was very sympathetic towards my mum and her illness. But over time, as I began to notice that in some ways, she seemed to enjoy being sick, my feelings started to harden. Eventually, I was no longer capable of feeling sorry for her; if anything, I found her to be a complete inconvenience. I stopped caring, stopped actively helping, and didn't want her to get better. I was happy if she sat in any type of pain, if that pain was even real, as this meant that she was feeling an inch of the internal pain I'd felt every day since I was a child.

In the year leading up to me going no contact, both parents experienced severe physical challenges. Dad had undergone a big surgery to completely remove his pancreas as they had found potential cancerous cells, and Mum experienced two falls due to losing her balance. I was the only one living at home. I was the only one there to witness all of this on a day-to-day basis. This was probably one of the hardest years of my life, but I knew my resilience ran deep. As I was the only one at home, I knew that I would be cornered into helping them. I had to maintain my sanity. Let me correct any thoughts you may have as the reader that I come off as selfish during these times. When I've never received any support from my parents when I needed care, what in my right mind would make me think it's acceptable to care for them? I just didn't have that empathy for them; I saw them as evil. During this time, I was forced to drive back and forth from the home to the hospital, taking my mum to visit my dad. These visits felt pointless, forced, and uncomfortable to me. My mum would act like the doting wife, bringing scraps of food for my dad and pressuring him to eat them instead of the hospital meals. He'd occasionally refuse, and I'd be left dealing with two emotionally immature parents — bickering in the hospital, dismissing the nurses and staff, and acting as if I weren't even there. Their behaviour felt shameless. A couple of times, I was at the hospital at the same time as my brother and his wife. They visited purely to save face, knowing that, in my parents' old age, they needed to at least be *seen* to care. They didn't want their names removed from the will — something my mum had been threatening us with since we were children. I watched my brother, confused in his emotions for our dad, acting like he was genuinely upset and worried about him being in the hospital. I found the whole act insincere. How has he forgotten all the abuse he's witnessed — and lived through — at the hands of this man? As for his wife, I believe she lacked both integrity and empathy. To me, she treated life with our family like a game, collecting brownie points where she could. But in reality, she couldn't give a shit.

They say you have to reach the darkest, lowest points in your life — rock bottom, they call it. But once you survive it, it can feel like you've been recreated by the sun itself, its rays pulsing through your entire body. You feel reborn.

2

COWARD

I like to refer to this part of my story as *Coward*. As humans, I feel we should all agree that any form of abuse is a cowardly act. This could be abuse to other humans, abuse to animals, or even sometimes abuse to yourself.

This is when good-natured people get abused. Helpless, defenceless people get abused. Their vulnerability is played with, and the abuse is rife. These are cowards who do this. A parent can shape a whole child's future. But it takes a courageous child to navigate the world and build an internal moral compass when their caregivers create a physically and emotionally unsafe environment. What is the child meant to do? Those types of people are the most cowardly in my eyes. They don't have the strength to face their responsibilities. They don't dare to protect, and they certainly can't hold love for themselves or their own child.

When arguments got too vocal, and my mum was realising that she wasn't getting her way of controlling me — by silencing me or shutting me down — being thrown out of the house was always their go-to plan. At first, it started off as a threat. And that threat would put my emotions into overdrive. I'd be crying, asking them to stop, and telling them that they couldn't possibly kick me out of the house over a petty argument. In my parents' minds, what was petty to me was deadly serious for them — and what was serious to me, they saw as petty. This is how complex the narcissistic abuse was. My dad would even offer to pack my things in a black bin bag and get rid of me.

Being thrown out of the house was something I then began to get used to; the more I had to experience it, the more I knew what to do. I would be able to sense the way an argument between Mum and Dad would go. I could sense the changes in Dad's stature — the way Mum kept egging him on to kick me out, saying, "Let's see who in the world would take you in. The world out there is cruel". I grew to learn that the outside world was hard, but nowhere near as cruel as the world I was living in at the house on Asquith Boulevard. Where did I used to go, you ask me? One of the times I was able to rent student accommodation, I was lucky enough to live with an ex-boyfriend of mine and his dad at their home for a long time. Unfortunately, when we split up, I had no choice but to return home. Another time, I lived with my brother for six months, and once again, I found myself surrounded by people with no good intentions. He told me, "Toilet roll is expensive, so you either need to pay more rent or go back". Everything was always transactional with my brother. Every interaction had a price to pay, and every offering was a "What can you do for me?" scenario. But when you are a uni student with only a part-time job, how are you expected to pay rent for a price that is too high – knowing damn well you'd have to return to the hell hole that was labelled *home*? Another coward to add to the equation. Because truly, an older brother is known in society as a protector, a defender, and someone you can rely on. A brother will speak to your overwhelmed emotions with a type of logic that can hold compassion. A person who you can go to for a respite from the world — to be silly and misbehave, as brother-and-sister sibling relationships usually do. Unfortunately, I did not possess that with my brother as we got older. In fact, in the later years, it felt like I had no brother at all. He vanished and disappeared without a trace.

Most people won't know this about me, but loud noises like bangs, a balloon popping, or something falling off the kitchen cabinet literally freaks me the hell out. It's a bit odd, as this trauma response only started once I went no contact. I physically feel scared — almost on high alert — because I don't believe it was just a normal noise. Those types of loud noises take me back to that household. They take me back to my dad's relentless anger and my mum's screaming. Those sounds will haunt me forever.

A lot of the story revolves around Mum — how it's *her* house and how she holds the reins over all the puppets living under her roof. But I do not, and will not, forget the abuse that was inflicted on me by my dad.

Let's talk about dads — protectors, defenders, and providers. The ones who offer a place of solace in hard times. A man who can lead and go about his business. The dad I had did not embody a single trait of a conventional dad. The days I have spent racking my brain, wondering if my failed romantic relationships stem from the trauma I carry from him. As women, we will always be in the firing line when it comes to men — but mine was different. I knew from a young age that I never had my dad's love, and that left a massive hole in my heart as I got older.

One of the coldest, emptiest souls I have ever known in my lifetime — a man who has no interest in his daughters, living in fear that they will turn out exactly like his wife. With that fear, he becomes dark, and his energy turns darker than ever as he goes about his days sulking, silent, and living in despair. How would a young girl even begin to understand the complexities that run through her dad's mind? All she knows is that she craves emotion, security, love, and affection. One of the last phrases Dad said to me before I left that house was, "You will leave me now in my old age, really?" I looked him dead in the eyes and said firmly, "Yes, I will". There was no wavering in my decision to leave. But to support him in his old age, when all my life I've been kicked to the curb by my own dad who didn't care if I was dead or alive? Well, there was no way in hell I'd be caring for him.

The treatment from my dad would usually begin with aggressive shouting in my face, questioning if I was mentally unstable — whether I spoke back or stayed silent. He'd approach me with eyes filled with rage, and I never knew if he'd kill me there and then, or if today I'd be spared. Slamming doors, smashing remote controls, shutting cupboard doors with force — and his favourite: slamming the front door and leaving the house. He would do this after nearly every argument with Mum, and he would not return for hours on end. I'd look out the window and watch him walk away. This wasn't him walking away from his wife, it was him walking away from his kids and showing me that when things get tough and he hasn't got the courage, he will walk — regardless of the situation.

There was a hell of a lot of screaming, shouting, things being thrown, doors being slammed, things being smashed — running up the stairs in fear, trying to get into a safe room — that occurred frequently in that household. I find it difficult to take myself back to that place, as it was when I was the most scared. My dad, the aggressor in most of those situations, would not be afraid to threaten to get a knife out and kill his wife. He has thrown suitcases down the staircase before as she's been shouting at the bottom of the steps, in hopes he'd crush her. He's used a slipper — or *champal*, the Gujarati word — to smack my sister. He's walked out of the family home slamming the door. He's been up against the wall whilst my brother has confronted him. He's told me he'd "break my legs in half" if I didn't be quiet. This man may represent himself as quiet and calm to others, but he really is far from it. He has a wicked temper.

There are certain laws in the UK now that mean men or women can be prosecuted for domestic violence even if it doesn't become physical. Threatening behaviour — like breaking objects in front of someone, or coercive and controlling behaviour — is still classed as domestic violence. If I had known this and had the courage when I was younger, I could have reported both parties for domestic violence, actually.

That's an even more saddening thought — not only were my parents narcissistic, enabling, and neglectful, but now both of them, if not definitely my dad, would fall under the category of causing domestic violence. You can't write this, can you? Oh, wait — I actually am.

We had to pick up the pieces when he would walk out, as Mum would switch into victim mode. This mode looked like fake tears, self-pity, and — because she had enraged him so much — a sudden need for company. She wanted us to feel sorry for her. I spent days sitting by her side as a child, telling her he would return, that he hadn't left us for good, and that I was there to help. This was the yo-yo situation I was faced with — always having to parent the parent. I felt like an outsider, lost in the world, unable to comprehend why I had to endure so much suffering.

Once again, this was all I knew. And then, as I got older, I started dating men who wouldn't stick around when times got tough. And trust me — there were many days when I was juggling life, myself, and the abuse, and I needed support. But I never received it from these men. This was a direct mirror of what Dad showed me. He showed me that he couldn't show resilience, that his needs came before anyone else's, and that he was the only one allowed to blow up like an explosive bomb, leaving us to pick up the pieces and shattering our feelings to the ground.

The biggest problem with Dad wasn't his anger, his cold heart, or his lack of emotional availability. It was his sheer ability to back his wife when she wanted to inflict pain on her children. It was the mockery in his words, the strength in his support for his wife, and the hiding behind the monster he married. That was the scariest part of all. Days and years would go by, and she would still treat him the same — talk to him with such disgust and disappointment — and he would take it all. He even convinced himself he was crazy, dumb, stupid, and a nobody. I knew from a young age that his crippling low self-esteem would cause problems. This black shadow of a dad, with no self-confidence, no self-esteem, and dark energy, was still living. And that's something I'll never understand. *How was he bearing all of this?* I used to think. *How can he live in such suffering?* There was a point in my mid-20s when I felt deeply sorry for him and wondered if there would ever be a way out for him. Fortunately, I began to realise quite quickly that he wanted to stay put. All the times he slammed doors and walked out were just acts — a performance. He enjoyed playing this twisted Joker-and-Harley-Quinn duo with his rotten wife. It was all just a game to him — a narrative he'd written in his head, that his life was meant to end up like this. And, somehow, he enjoyed it.

In one way, he'd always been looking for a place to fit in the family — and because she was the one who controlled the entire family dynamic, he found his place as the enabler. The way he would torment my sister as soon as his wife clicked her fingers. The way he would add to the rage whenever she said so. The neglect he showed us whenever his wife's narcissistic ego was burned. Another empty shell of a human who sold his soul to the devil.

The shouting would never stop — the constant rage, the anger, the disgust, the distaste. I felt it all — and yet, at the same time, I dissociated from it for my sanity.

Creeping down the stairs, pausing halfway as she shouted nonstop about the terrible things she felt about me. That I was a whore. A stupid, lost girl. A person who didn't deserve to live. That I should drink cooking oil and kill myself. These words, like poison, seeped into my psyche. Yet I stood frozen — traumatised and in pain — in the middle of the staircase, trying to remember that I am none of the things she was shouting at me. But where do I go? Not upstairs, not down — these rages lasted for hours. She would paint the house with that vile language, slamming doors as she moved from the living room to the kitchen. To know that you are that hated by a parent who feels the need to spread insults all over the house is one of those feelings you internalise. And then, even when the parent isn't around, those voices still echo in your head.

I entered the living room, and the walls that once held her insults threw them back out at me. I went to the kitchen, and all the appliances started whispering what she had told them about me. My safety was outside — in the trees, the parks, the green grass. Anywhere she hadn't yet spewed her hatred. Let's not dismiss the shadow in black. His rage exploded like a volcano and would have surely reached the ends of the garden. The words — that he wanted to smash my face in, that I was an idiot, that I was always at fault. The slander he used would rile her up, as they enjoyed inflicting this abuse together. The pair of them were evil to the core, playing their children like instruments just so they could dance to the sound of their torment.

I'd spend my whole life thereafter searching for peace, trying to quieten the noises in my head and reminding myself: *this is not me*. As I got older, I realised my only duty of care was to myself — and to the younger Sonam. There's a saying: physical scars will heal, but mental ones never will. When I think back to my childhood and teenage years — the years that were supposed to be precious — I remember how I used to deeply reflect on the world I lived in. And now, I let it sink in that my mind was forged through trauma.

How would Sonam really see the world? How do others see the world? Why do I carry so much emotion when I've never been nurtured? Do I just let my mind float away?

How does my soul cope with such heartache? Is it because any little glimpse of peace or happy emotion I've felt, I keep with me, wrapped up in a wooden box with a gold clasp, and hidden away deep inside a private place in my soul that I've carved out for it? Is that where I store all those small glimmers of hope?

The expectations from a narcissistic parent are huge, as nothing is ever good enough or acceptable for them. Unless you are the golden child, those expectations stick with you and begin to mould you into someone you are not.

For a long period, I would hide away in my room and look out my window with big dreams — that one day, things would change. That one day, life would suddenly be perfect. I'd spend so much time reevaluating every decision I've ever made, knowing deep in my heart how my soul wanted to speak. I didn't find the words to do this until recently in my life. But can you imagine — knowing who you want to be and how you want to live, but every time you look in the mirror, you're surrounded by your abusers? So instead, you cast out an empty shell so they don't see who you really are. Because the minute they catch a glimpse of your true self, they'll scrutinise every part of that person. They'll instantly paint flaws and project their disappointment the moment they can. Sonam — who is she? Who is she, deep down? She's a carefree, fun-loving person. Someone who wants to experience life and feel peace in the same breath. She's a girl who is extremely intelligent and seeks to understand human connection. A girl who enjoys being around people but can also happily sit alone. She smiles when her loved ones are happy. She feels joy when she can speak freely. Sonam has an abundance of love to give — to her friends, her loved ones, and her partner. How did I become so empathetic? How did I not let the world force me to have a bitter heart? I think only the Universe knows the answer.

In this part of the story, we fast forward to when I've gone no contact with the narc parents — and a few others. I'm boarding an evening flight from London Heathrow to Changi Airport, Singapore. This trip was meant to be the most exhilarating one yet, especially as I was splitting my two weeks away between Singapore and Bali. Unfortunately, the tone of the trip turned out to be very different from what I had originally set it as.

Ever since I was a little girl, the time I spent away from *home* was the best feeling for me. Staying at my sister's, sleeping over at friends' houses, attending festivals, joining my friend on her *Christian weekends* — which is a story for another chapter — but honestly, as long as I came back to my own bed after the sun had set, that was all I needed for a good day.

I had a massive awakening during that two-week trip to Asia. I felt chronic anxiety for about 90% of the time I was there. It wasn't anyone's fault, and it had nothing to do with the location — it was all me. My soul was breaking and bending as I finally began to understand the trauma I'd lived with my entire life... and tried to make sense of it. The days I felt vulnerable and cried were because I was homesick. This girl had never — I mean *never* — felt homesick in her entire life. And now, at nearly 30, she was. How incredibly disturbing.

There's a difference between missing your own bed, as they say when people are away from home a bit too long, and not wanting to leave home in the first place. Because I knew, the minute I stepped on that 12-hour flight, I didn't want to go. Now, you ask what *home* consisted of for me. It was the people I truly loved and had been creating deep bonds with. It was the cosy little apartment that gave me warmth, security, and peace. It was the mundane routines I'd created for myself — routines that weren't mundane anymore. They were peaceful and necessary because I was finally looking after myself. For once I was wholeheartedly looking after myself. Instead of escaping, this holiday was more of a reminder that I now have a home to go back to.

I'm overlooking the Marina on a gorgeously hot day, but I can't help feeling triggered — just five minutes earlier, I'd interacted with two elderly Indian parents who, without a doubt, reminded me how much I wasn't loved by my own. They were kind. They were sweet. And most importantly, they had travelled all this way to visit their son — while my parents didn't even know if I was dead or alive. That hurt. It felt like a stab to the chest. But what could I do about that now? I reminded myself that good, loving parents exist. Just not in my life.

I had many revelations on this trip of a lifetime, but all I could think about in the back of my mind was how much I had loved creating this little life for myself back at home. I finally felt I had a home. Sonam did it for her. On the trip, it was hard. I had to mask in front of a lifelong friend, and I had to take in the beautiful scenery while wishing I had my people with me — a little bit of home with me. I felt confused. I kept thinking back, feeling lost and insecure. This wasn't the Sonam I had known for all these years. The girl-like wonder she always had — the light wasn't shining as bright this time.

Even though this may depict that I had a terrible trip mentally, I felt it was totally necessary — and exactly what I needed at the start of 2024 — for me to lean into who I was authentically becoming, aside from my trauma. The truth is, I can be halfway across the world and still be healing. Healing is never linear. But as long as I can express my feelings, then I know I'm one step closer to healing, bit by bit.

Bali is an incredible place. It has a different, unique type of energy when you are there. I was able to resonate with this island so deeply that I would return in a heartbeat. Everyone seemed to be healing, surrendering, and evolving. The friendliest of smiles came from strangers, and there are many places to practice gratitude. This is what made me feel that there was more to life than the suffering I'd known; that I could change things for myself. And that might mean starting afresh. As humans, we do have this unfortunate ability to stay very comfortable where we are. We even accept that situations and people are normal, even when they are not, just to avoid rocking the boat. I say to hell with that. Rock the boat. Rock it hard and be loud with it. Who deserves this life more than you?

3

LIAR

A key memory of my abuse — now, as an adult child of a narcissist — was when an argument between me and my dad sparked a deep emotion of terror inside me. This shook me as I didn't realise I still felt fearful of my dad, but when I was in the downstairs living room, hands physically shaking, out of breath, and in sweats, I knew in that moment that things needed to change. This had to stop. I was 28 years old, and I was quivering like a little girl.

This started when my mum went into the hospital after a fall. She had to stay there for a number of weeks to have repairs done on a hip replacement she had many years ago. I remember feeling anxious at this time because I knew all the attention was going to be on my mum. She would sink into the role of a victim — a role of someone who is completely helpless — and cast a dark shadow over everyone around her so that we would be manipulated to feel sorry for her. I already knew this agenda was coming from my mum, so I did what any child of a narc parent does and tried to tiptoe around her emotions. At home, it was just me and my dad. He went into his robotic routine of being available for his wife 24/7, but I knew this wouldn't last long. One day, after he returned from the hospital, after visiting her and being by her side all day, something in him shifted. He was dark and full of rage, and the only person he was going to take that out on was me, his daughter. By this point, I had my guard up and pressed record on my Samsung Galaxy Flip 5 (a brilliant mobile phone, by the way. It can be secretly concealed in a pocket, or even in your hand, recording). As soon as I hit record, I approached him and asked if he was okay. He began explaining how his wife was a bitch, how she was never happy with him, and how he could never do anything right in her eyes. I asked him to calm down, but this just made him worse. He slammed the chest of drawers in his bedroom and said that I was also the cause of all his pain. That I was a *"fucking bitch"* that needed to die, along with my sister and brother-in-law. He then said, and I quote, that he wanted to get a shotgun and shoot us all dead. At this moment, I knew my safety was being compromised, so I decided to retreat to my room. His shouting, swearing, and aggression only got worse, and I had to just numb myself from the pain of hearing all of this in the next room.

When this got too much, I ran downstairs and hid in the part of the living room that felt the safest. And that's when little Sonam came to the surface, saying she couldn't handle this anymore. That she's done with the on-and-off years of not feeling safe anywhere. The paranoia, the fear, the sadness — she couldn't carry it anymore. She was pleading with me, as the adult, to figure something out. To leave. This was then the start of my next journey.

At this time, I was engaged to someone — a person who is now just someone that I used to know. When I decided to open up to them and share my whole truth, with evidence of text messages and voice recordings of the abuse, I was completely shut down. He didn't want to believe me. The lack of awareness and misinformation he had about the situation put me back into a victim mindset. I was pleading for him to understand, but he didn't. I ended the engagement very shortly after this time, which meant all hell broke loose at home. On reflection, that ex was a young boy living in an adult man's body. He would have never held space for me to open up further about my abuse. He was selfish and lacked the awareness to comprehend that abuse even happens. Not many days went by without him telling me to put on a brave face and crack on with the wedding plans — all to appease his 400 guests. Hindsight is a beautiful thing. I now realise that he and I only got together, brief as it was, because of my parents' encouragement. He represented everything they'd always wanted. More supply. More points to boost their egos in society. I didn't love him the way I wanted to. It was all a setup — an act of convenience. And I fell for it. Until I didn't.

I moved into my sister's house to be safe from all the pain. I used work as an escape and tried to ignore all the toxic, loud voices in my head. However, as soon as I ended my engagement, my mum went on her last and final rampage before we cut her off — and oh boy, did she go on. The streams of missed calls, the vile text messages, and foul voicemails she left not just on my phone, but on my sister's, brother-in-law's, and even my niece's. This woman was not going to stop. As soon as I was born, she wanted to bury my soul into the ground — but I didn't let her. I had my pillars of support by my side that kept me rising above the ground. A narcissist will begin to crumble when they feel their self-image, reputation, and ego begin to break — and that's exactly what happened when I ended things. She didn't see it coming. She had to find out from my ex's mother that I had ended the engagement, and that sent her spiralling. But this brought me a sense of achievement. I thought it was about time she was unable to control the narrative. They do say that when a victim tries to leave an abusive relationship, it is possibly one of the most dangerous times of their lives — and I believe that to be true in my situation, even though this was a parent-daughter relationship. My mum blackmailed me, saying that she and my dad would commit suicide. She twisted the story to my nieces, trying to influence them. Telling them, and I quote, to "correct their parents" for supporting me and letting me live with them while I found housing. My nieces were only teenagers, and they knew full well they couldn't dictate anything in their own parents' house. My mum began to see that these manipulation tactics weren't working and accepted the fact that I would be staying with my sister. She threatened to throw all of my clothes into bin bags and dump them on the front lawn — just so people could see I'd been chucked out. Then she gave me a deadline for when I had to come and collect my things. Narcissists will discredit that you even have belongings and possessions. They will damage and destroy as they lack basic respect for you and your things. I had to do this at a time that was most suitable for me, when I was mentally ready to deal with them again.

The day I decided to collect my things, I remember the weather was predicted to rain, but I had committed to this day and knew I couldn't back out. I was dressed in joggers and a hoodie, gym trainers on, and I was ready to go in like a military operation. But to my surprise, the weather was warmer than expected, and I feel it was a sign from the Universe, as this meant I didn't need to carry any soggy cardboard boxes anywhere. When a girl is doing all this alone, sometimes she just needs a break, you know? I went into the house and grabbed as many things of importance as possible, but I had to leave behind a lot of my books; that was the saddest part. The possessions that brought me the most comfort, I had to leave behind. The narcissist will make it difficult for you to leave, as the majority of the time, they have stripped you of all identity and self-worth, making it emotionally hard to leave. I was in a blessed position to have the support around me, and my mental health was at a point where I knew the only way was to leave. One lesson I've learnt in life is that once you stick to something, you better not look back.

I like to call this part: Liar

My mum was a pathological liar, her life was based upon lies. It's ironic, isn't it really? She has lived her entire life making up lie after lie — or what she likes to call *stories*. But she then had a daughter who decided not to *make up* her story, but to explain her life as a true story, with as much raw emotion and honesty as possible. So, thanks Mum — you think you can tell stories? Well, I can tell them a hell of a lot better than you, and at least mine are true.

She's been caught out in plenty of lies before, lost family members, friends, and others due to her lying. A fraud can't stay a fraud for too long, can they. The biggest mistake she made was that she became sloppy in her lying and game playing. It's almost like a top athlete who feels they'll never be defeated and are at the top of their game because they've spent decades playing — that was my mum. They fail to realise, however, that younger, fresher, more skilled athletes can come into the picture and steal the medal in a split second. Don't ever get too comfortable, they say. She had underestimated me.

One day, Mum was up to her usual tricks and decided it was time to cause trouble and disrupt the household. She had called me downstairs and asked me to sit down in front of her as she had something to share with me. She knew that I used my room as a retreat, and that made her feel powerful as she had full control over the whole house. I mean it's quite reflective of a child's behaviour to be up in their room all day, that's why she loved the power of having to call me down as if it was a demand. I came downstairs, ready to tackle the bullshit that came my way, but I was too hellbent on keeping the peace in the home. My tactic was to always make it seem that she wasn't getting to me and that I was too busy to sit and listen to her rant for any longer than 5 minutes.

This day was different. She sat me down in front of my dad to explain that my sister had called her earlier that morning and was causing a fuss, trying to stir the pot and talk about others in the family — mainly me. Now, my brain already knew this was utter bullshit, because my sister would never do such a thing. We had a unity of hatred for our mum and a united bond of love for one another.

I asked my mum why she would do this out of the blue, and she said she didn't know — that she was disgusted by my sister's behaviour. I sat silently, but had my finger hovering over the record button in WhatsApp, ready to send the evidence over to my sister.

I asked a further question: "Well, what do you want me to do about this?" And because I'd phrased this in a tone my mum disagreed with, she completely flipped and began shouting. That's when I hit record on the phone and was able to send over to my sister everything that was said in that argument.

My mum shouted that she needed me to get involved — to call my sister and have a go at her for bitching about other people. The horror that took over my face... I knew my mum was only doing this to get a reaction out of me. I refused her request, and that's when she got even worse with her shouting and verbal abuse.

This triggered my dad, and — SHOWTIME — it was time for him to play his role. His shouting was even louder than my mum's. They were both hellbent on making sure their other daughter was dragged through the dirt.

I was hellbent on protecting my sister at all costs. I kept refusing, telling them their parenting was horrendous and that my life was going to be much better without them.

My dad said that if I followed in my sister's footsteps, then my life would be cursed and it would rapidly go downhill.

I pause in writing and smile to myself, as the next year of my life without them was the start of the best years of my life.

I decide enough is enough and walk away from the argument, hearing the shouting and swearing slowly decrease. I had a plan to catch her out on her lie, after I'd sent my sister the recorded voice note, she rang me and we discussed how crazy our parents were. My sister had even taken a screenshot of her call log from the day and showed me, so I knew there was never any doubt that she hadn't called our mum. That sparked an idea in my mind that I needed to check my mum's call logs, so I waited till the early evening to go and approach her again, when I knew she had called some of her friends and got her validation and ego trip from them.

I showed fake interest "Oh Mum, did you manage to connect your wireless Bluetooth headphones to your phone? I can help you if you are struggling, honestly". She looked up at me from having her focus glued to Facebook on her iPad and said, "Yes, I need them, my hands hurt too much having to hold up the phone when I'm talking to my friends". I smiled and nodded and went over to her drawer, took out the headphones, and then asked for her mobile, which she handed over. See this is where narcs are fucking idiots as once again her attention was off her daughter - who as a child would have cried and felt so unloved by the lack of attention, this time is utterly pleased she is being left alone - I could go into detective mode and get my evidence. I sat on the sofa opposite her chair so she couldn't see what I was doing and went straight to her call log from today. Shock - there were no calls from my sister at all today, but not just today, for several days her name was not on the call history of the mobile. I calmly set up the Bluetooth headphones for her, inside I was seething - how dare she lie to my face, in fact, make up a story so she could have fun and cause drama. All this time my cortisol levels in my body were spiking up, making me feel on edge.

I knew I had to take my chance and call her out on her shit there and then, so that's exactly what I did. "Mum, are you sure my sister called you earlier today?" She looked at me, perplexed. "Yes, Sonam, why?" I couldn't believe how stupid she thought I was. "Mum, come on, I know she didn't call you, did she. There's no need to make things up". I genuinely spoke to her in the most patronising way as if she were a child. She didn't answer, as she was confused. This is how narcs convince themselves a lie is the truth. "Look, I can see from your phone that there is not a single call from her in a very long time". Immediately when faced with the facts, my mum went into a fit of rage, saying that I'd invaded her privacy and questioning what sort of daughter I am not to believe my mum at face value. But come on, you tell me, how can you trust the person who hurts you the most? In her usual fashion, she began crying, moving around in her chair as if she were a little child having a tantrum and needing to express this through every fibre of her body. I felt a sense of power knowing I had technology on my side, but it made me reflect on the days when she could've used the same lie in the past — when smartphones weren't around and it wouldn't have been so easy to catch her out. It made me feel for my sister, who had to live through that generation.

On the subject of lying, I want to explain the impact this can have on larger groups of people who are heavily involved with the narc. Chinese whispers, rumours and the like are different to something called the smear campaign. A smear campaign is when the narc recruits a set of people that she knows will do her dirty work for her, or flying monkeys, as they are called in the narc terminology guide. A flying monkey was my dad, my brother, and my uncle in America. Funny how they are all men, I will go into the manipulation a woman narc can do to men a bit later on. These men decided that they wanted to blindly pick the side of their devoted wife, decent mum, and amazing sister. As my mum spent decades preserving her self-image and reputation, it was difficult for anyone to speak up and share the truth. It felt as if my sister's and I's voices were tiny, like a newborn babbling to speak, going up against all these non-believers. Our brother came at his smear campaign from a slightly different angle — he didn't flat-out speak negatively about us to the family, but then again, he didn't speak positively either. A true non-believer or ignorant soul to the abuse he's witnessed as a child growing up. He explained to me and my sister that he would take a *non-judgmental* approach to the situation and that we have to do what is best for us, and that we should "stick to our decision". That's a sign of someone who wants the *mess* to go away, the *evidence* to dissipate. Turns out, shortly after that interaction with him, he decided to cut contact with us and faded away into the hands of our abusive parents. Either he was given an ultimatum, or he just didn't see what happened to us as abuse because he clings to the idea of coming from a *perfect* family. I will never know.

My uncle in America, now he only felt obliged to get involved when quote "She's my only family left". There we go, another person clinging to a false hope for a family. He didn't want to acknowledge how damaging and toxic his sister has been, not only to his nieces but his own wife and family in the past. Why do we surrender to the most evil of people? To keep the *peace*, to protect ourselves or our selfish, greedy needs? I feel my uncle did all three. Unfortunately, no one sees us as children anymore; they see us as grown women who are causing *drama*. When we sat our uncle down and told him all about the abuse, and showed him the recordings and text messages, he was surely shocked and showed disgust at how his own sister had gossiped about him and his own children for years. However, he robotically went back to his old ways and decided he would rather try to prove his sister's innocence and his niece's guilt. Fast forward a year, and it's been revealed that he is utterly embarrassed and ashamed of his actions. That he contributed to the pain we went through. He's still confused about where to place his sister, but because he's been confronted by his own family, he knows morally he's stuck. To uncover a line of abuse is difficult; the family members who enable an abuser become trapped emotionally as well, because when they knew there had been wrongdoing in the family, they turned a blind eye and didn't want to step out of their comfort zone to help. If a family falls apart because a certain member decided to leave, that should give you all the proof that the family itself was more like a cult — with people being controlled and living in fear, rather than a true support system that would let people come and go as freely as they pleased.

4

SYMBOLIC

It's quite symbolic that I can write about the process of change in chapter 4. Number 4 in spirituality means stability, balance, and foundations. In 2024, I truly found this - interesting, as I had spent my entire life searching for stability and peace, and then all of a sudden, it was presented to me in the form of a beautiful apartment. Small in size, but full of character, as the building had been around since the 1700s. It was tucked away in a peaceful nook, and my apartment was number 4 out of the 5 apartments in the building. Quaint, quiet and safe, that's how I've grown to know number 4. Let's look at a few other synchronicities of number 4. It is also the same number as my sister's house, another safe haven for me. I met my kindred spirit after 3 failed relationships (we can't really count the one when I was 18, but hey, it makes 4 doesn't it). I also went to visit my psychic on the 4th of September 2024. I left my old job on the 4th of the month after nearly 4 years at the same company. This number is even tattooed on me, and believe it or not, it is the fourth tattoo I have on my body. I honestly couldn't get more connected to the number if I tried, right?

Before I was blessed with apartment no 4 and I would say my healing journey began, I had to go through a phase during which I was living at my sister's house. This part was crucial for us moving forward as a family, as this is where the decision was made to go no contact with my parents. At this point, I'd ended my engagement, moved out of the abusive home with a couple of bags and was due to start a new role in the company I worked for. This was extremely hard, as usually I was good at separating the two lives I would live, but this time I couldn't, and it felt like everything was collapsing into one big mess. I couldn't keep a brave face on at work for too long and crumbled, briefly telling my manager about what I was suffering. She was as supportive as she could be, but I still didn't want my life to completely fall apart. My sister and the family encouraged me that a new start at work could be positive, allowing time for us to build our lives from the ground up. We all went through the same but different trauma together for the next couple of months til the end of 2023. When I started living at my sisters, my mum absolutely hated it because she knew she was losing the controlling grip she had all her life. She knew that my sister was strong, my brother-in-law was fiercely protective and that she wouldn't be able to penetrate through to us. One of the messages explained that when she was pregnant with me, my sister, in a fit of rage, kicked her in the stomach. Now, believe me — it sounds shocking, doesn't it? But I collated each and every piece of evidence, with screenshots and my previous recordings, all in one album. We then shared this evidence around the family so we all had backup. How could a 70-something-year-old woman want to plot her daughters against each other so badly that she would make up such a cruel lie? My sister never even touched our mum when she was pregnant with me, my mum never went to the hospital for any injuries, and I was born a healthy baby, so why would she say this? This accusation was out of spite — she wanted to try any form of emotional blackmail to get me to return home and cut ties with my sister. Little did she know, it was only making us stronger. One night in particular, we all sat in the living room and awaited the hateful line-up of messages to come through, and that's exactly what happened. Our mum was on a rampage and continuously sent messages every hour or so from 10 am until 11 pm that day. The messages even came through from my dad's phone, but we knew that the vile language was from our mum. In between ignoring her messages, she began to leave voicemails. These voicemails were a plea for help — she was begging my sister and brother-in-law to release me from their home and send me back, as if I were a prisoner. She also used my dad as a prop, getting him to be aggressive on the phone, shouting and saying he thinks so low of us — that we are scum and he never expected this kind of behaviour from his *son-in-law*. I wanted to explain the mask-switching that a narcissistic person does. For quite some time, I only ever heard positive words about my brother-in-law, especially when it was in front of other people. And now, because he no longer serves his narc in-laws, he's damaged goods, discarded, and a low-life scumbag. See how quickly that mask can switch? I can't begin to explain the trauma that came with experiencing all of this, the highs and lows of emotion and the uncertainty of what would happen next. One part I can share with you is that when you see a narc for who they really are, it's like the rose-tinted glasses fall off and smash to the ground, and there's no way you can unsee them for who they are. This is how we felt about our parents, so with that, the decision was made to block them on all contact forms, which meant blocking her access on social media, blocking her phone calls, text messages, WhatsApp messages and video calls. Each one of us in the family did this, and as soon as we discovered that's all it took to cut them out, we never looked back.

I want to share with you my catalyst for change in this chapter. Physically, I was deteriorating, rapidly losing weight, my skin was dull and lifeless, and my hair was falling out more than usual. I could feel my body ache in places they hadn't before, and was even having a menstrual bleed way before my period date; these all felt like trauma responses to my body. On reflection, this was me shedding my skin like a snake does as something new was about to blossom. I was going through the phases where I felt my world had fallen apart, because let's face it, it had, but not in the way that I needed to be concerned about. I was used to feeling like a prisoner in my own safe space, a place I called home. This wasn't my world falling apart, this was actually my life falling into place. Don't get me wrong, things were unsettled for months before any sense of stability began, and that was due to a few setbacks when trying to find a suitable place to move into after my sisters. I remember the days I was slowly losing hope because I wasn't getting the right location or place, and having to pull an application for an apartment that had complications — it was still in the process of being built, and the timeline was uncertain as to when it would be finished.

The song *Fighter* by Christina Aguilera plays in the background as I write this part of the chapter. Fitting as I was not prepared to give up, and my chosen family was not going to give up on me. This is where my intuition started kicking back in. They do say that children of narc abuse tend to have special gifts given to them by the Universe, and I believe my intuition was slowly unblocking once the poison left. An apartment popped up when I was scrolling one evening, and it was in the perfect location. I banked it as the one I'd revisit. I was desperately trying to get my money and belongings back from this other apartment first, before I could move forward with this new apartment.

Number 4 waited for me, stayed on the app Rightmove, and when I went back to arrange a viewing, I impressed the landlord from the off, and within a couple of days the apartment was mine to rent. I remember I was overjoyed as I could finally move on with my life and move forward. I do now believe the saying, *what is meant for you, will always be*. I'd organised a van to move all my belongings from one place to another, packed the remainder of my belongings from my sister's house and was able to leave with my head held high. It didn't take me too long to settle into Number 4, and before I knew it, I wasn't always completely alone like I had pictured I would be for years.

The Universe sent its second blessing of the year, in the form of a partner. The most out of the blue connection, but a connection that is for lifetimes to come. This time, however, I felt I had created a home for myself. I was a steady anchor in my own life, so having anyone else come into it was just a bonus. It's funny how one of my mum's last curses to me was "Go find the right man now, which you never will". I'd have loved to say to her "Be careful what you wish for, bitch". As the exact opposite happened, and I indeed did find the right man at the right time.

The combination of creating a long-lasting bond of love and a home in tow meant that I knew the Universe was pleased with me. I truly believe we have all been put onto this earth to face trials and tribulations, and not for a notion of a God, but for ourselves as individual souls. The cards that I was dealt with have been terrible from the beginning but the Universe was showing me signs and had previously shown me that if I just listen, just fucking listen to the Universe, it will deliver exactly what I needed. With this newfound awareness, I continued moving forward.

During this time, there were setbacks, there were many first times, and there was peace. That is the key word for this chapter: peace. Suffering from PTSD from my parents' attacks, I had many nightmares of being trapped back in the hellhole and that this new life was just a fantasy, like how I dreamed of when I was younger. The part of my subconscious couldn't believe that I had actually escaped; it wasn't registering that I did it. This is why narcissistic abuse keeps you stuck, it's like an invisible metal chain that keeps you attached and drags you to return back when you fear the unknown. I've grown to learn that the unknown isn't what I should be fearing, as it's safer than knowing the devil itself. I'd be waking up each morning within the first few months of my move, and granted, I was alone, I'd stare out of my apartment window and look out into the quaint village I lived in, and couldn't help but feel a sense of being out of place. Now, how does this make any sense? Well, let me tell you... When you know nothing but trauma and chaos, your mind clings to that space, it almost manipulates it so you become numb, and then numbness becomes your safety net. As I'm staring out the window, feeling like I don't belong, I remember the days when I was living in the hellhole and waking up to being screamed and shouted at. Can you imagine everyone else is starting their day making a brew and I am being shouted at as soon as I leave that bedroom, still in my pajama's. The parallel of that situation is unnerving. So as my body and mind were so attuned to that type of trauma, when I could actually stand and be present in my own kitchen overlooking the trees in the distance and sipping on my coffee, I couldn't believe my eyes and my body was adjusting to regulating calmer emotions first thing in the morning.

Now, the topic of children. I want to address this quite early on in the book because as a woman in her early 30s, my viewpoint on having children has always been a bit on and off. The reason for this is that I was in an unhealed trauma state for a very long time in my life. That trauma state said, *when I have kids, I can fill them with love, and that it will fill a void within myself.* Now I've come to learn that isn't the case, and the best healing tool is to fill my inner child with love. This will take patience, grace and forgiveness to myself, and I for sure don't want to rush this process as now I'm open to the Universe delivering, it will deliver if it be a child at the right time and place.

Letter to my inner child

Oh Sonam. The little girl who wanted to adore life, she was ready from day one to experience every bit of life and wanted it to be like how it was in the movies, I being the main character and going on this journey of life, making friends, having fun, finding your purpose and falling, deeply and madly in love with your hero who comes in shining armour. I am so sorry that you actually didn't become the main character in your story, you were neglected and abandoned with no one to play with or talk to. You were left hungry and in your room for hours on end whilst you watched your mum become the main character in the story, later realising she was the villain. You found comfort in books; this was your first friend and confidant, and you'd rather read about Harry Potter being the main character, as he reminded you of your home. A boy who lived, and that's what you wanted to do, was to be a girl who lived.

Days went on by, and so did years, and you developed a sense of happiness when you made friends, the innocence in you was never lost and you had a charming naivety about you. Unfortunately, you soon came to realise that sadness would become your new friend, as you became sad for a very, very long time. The warm tears rolled down your face as you looked at yourself in the mirror and cried quietly, as you knew that no one was coming to save you or care for you. Sadness trailed behind you when you went to school, sadness came into your dreams as you slept, and sadness even came to visit you when you were surrounded by the happiest of people. That was probably the saddest, as you knew happiness was an emotion you could only dream of but barely attain. When did this change for you? I would say when you were able to start to form an identity outside the pain, you were able to lock that pain away with a bolt and a key. This was a survival tactic for you once you became a teenager, but it would rear its ugly head when a boy appeared. Now I know younger me would have felt the same emotions as any hormonal teenage girl, but for me, this was different. I was actively looking for love, as I knew I didn't get any of this at home. So I searched with such a mature mindset for the boy who made me smile, made me laugh and felt safe at the time. Believe it or not, I encountered some nice boyfriends when I was young, the ones I liked always fancied me back, and I gave a lot into those relationships. I didn't have my father's love, so who else would young Sonam turn to? The problem wasn't necessarily the boys — it was when the relationships ended. Because let's face it, they had to — we were all young, in school, without a clue. *That's when my box of pain used to break away from its bolt. The pain would rip into my heart so deeply, the feelings of rejection, isolation and neglect. All of these emotions were created by the hands of your abusive parents. No one wanted little Sonam, I'd say to myself, and I'd be embarrassed and full of shame, and then would shut myself off from emotions for a while, but she was always a believer and never gave up on the idea of love even as an adult.*

Don't worry darling, we had to touch upon the teenage stage just a little, the readers need context of how you were not just as a child but as a young girl too. Back to you now, this letter is filled with shared experiences, the complexity of your emotions, and me sharing now as adult Sonam that everything did work out. It worked out better than you thought actually.

My therapist taught me the tools to stay connected to my inner child, and he highlighted the utmost importance, as without staying connected to our inner child, we will fail in our older age. Remembering painful memories of when I was a little girl helps me heal the adult I am now, as I can navigate through my triggers. I can now embrace my younger self as an entity that is linked to me but doesn't define me anymore. When we keep the channels of communication open with our younger selves, we can talk to them when they are feeling a certain way, be there for them as an adult figure which they never had. As I entered my 30s and so on, I felt more connected to my inner child than ever before. I would occasionally touch in with her and ask her how she's feeling, what she wanted to do today, wear together or eat together. I made a promise to myself that I was going to always put her first.

5

CELEBRATIONS

I begin this chapter only a few days after the celebration of *Diwali*. Now, in simple terms, Diwali is a worldwide celebration by the indian and non indian communities to celebrate the *welcoming of light*. I'm sure you can Google the historic definition if you want to, but for me, I want to explain Diwali the way I was brought up with it, and then the way I changed my viewpoint of Diwali once I got older.

Unfortunately, in the hellhole of a house, Diwali was greatly celebrated by my parents, especially my mum. She never looked to God on the days when she was causing abuse, manipulation, deceit and pain, but she looked to God on the days when she wanted validation, greed, and to feed her ego. How dare the Devil dance with God? Is what I used to think... My mum would decorate parts of the house with festive colours, materials, candles, and religious statues — or in Gujarati, we called them *Murtis*. I'd look at these statues blankly, because as much as I found them aesthetically pleasing, I didn't believe in them. I couldn't believe in what they were meant to be representing, as this never existed inside the family home. Year after year, the family would be expected to gather at my mum's house, light a candle, do a *pooja* which is a blessing ceremony where you fakely sit and smile for the pictures. Anyone who is truly in touch with their religion should know how it feels, right? Well, I used to feel nothing, a bleak emptiness inside that would at times be replaced by anger as I'd watch family members interact with each other, but to such a disingenuous degree. At this point, my mum would lap up all the attention she would get from posting her religious statue displays on Facebook, without even acknowledging that her own daughters were sat in the house, deeply hurting as no one would want to interact with us or care that we were even there. Our brother would attend for the sake of it, again, he didn't want to be there, you could tell from his face. My brother could never hide an expression on his face, but what was scary was that he could hide his emotions and the agenda that he and his wife were playing for many years. Then there came the subject of food, as my mum was a complete cheapskate, she would prepare the same frozen spring rolls and samosas that were in the freezer, which wouldn't have surprised me if they were from a few years ago. She would lie that she was unwell so can't cook any more, but the true reason was that she didn't care to feed people; she never really fed me when I was a child, why would she start now? The hardest part of these starters being served as main food at the house meant that my nieces and nephew would go on eating pasta with tomato ketchup as a meal substitute. Luckily, when my sister and brother-in-law clocked that the food was done half heartedly, they'd feed their kids before they came to the house, so they didn't go hungry.

My mum would then put on the victim mask and complain that she's had to stand and fry all the spring rolls and samosas in the kitchen, mind you, she had a special disability chair that she could sit opposite the stove to fry the food. You have to understand that the compassion, if any, we held for our mum was running slim as we knew she was a brilliant actor. Shortly after, she would complain for the rest of the evening about how worn out she was, and that the house would be a mess when everyone left. She would then proceed to put the pressure on me and my sister to clean the dishes in the kitchen. And believe me when I say — it wasn't about us being messy, it was merely the principle. Especially for my sister, who's older, as she ideally wanted to feel that when she returned to her parents' home, she wasn't made to feel like a servant on such an auspicious occasion. If we pushed back and said we'd clean the dishes later, our mum would give us a dagger of a look and begin to raise her voice — a signal that she was about to lose it. Again, why does everyone have to tread on eggshells around her? The control this woman had over the family was overwhelming, and it was either fight or flight mode when it came to disagreeing with her.

The evening would be over and I'd be back upstairs in my room, reflecting back it was always just a charade... a show for my mum and no one else's emotions ever mattered. We couldn't talk freely, I felt this deep, uncomfortable pit in my stomach and knew I would be judged for drinking a couple of glasses of wine. I never learnt about what Diwali actually was, what it meant and how it should be celebrated, no context or background, no showing love or wishing abundance for my family from my parents. So then I'd end my evening by looking at other people's Diwali's on social media, wondering what their days were like. To add, Christmas was even worse at the hellhole house, but I'll get to that one later.

Ah, religion, a very mixed topic of opinions, creates division and creates unity. My thoughts on religion — especially being a Hindu — is that I've had to do it my way, and my way only. When I was a teenager, I resonated with Christianity quite deeply too at one point, as my best friend in school was a devout Christian. I thought you had to be a Christian to feel love, welcomed and accepted. I'd attend days out with the church with my friend, and I'd spend all day feeling as though I belonged somewhere. This was true; there are some amazing people that existed within that church group, but it wasn't necessarily God that made them great, it was just them and the way they wanted to be held as an individual person. I toyed with the idea of converting to Christianity on and off throughout Secondary school, but then drifted off the idea when the reality of being a Christian didn't truly align with my soul's path. At that time, I didn't realise that I just needed healing, the wounds needed seeing to, not just covering up with using religion as a plaster.

Back to being a Hindu, so within the home, my mum would use our religion to instil fear into me; she would always say, "God is watching". It was bad enough that she was always watching my every move and interaction, now I had *God*. The weird thing was, even though she used this as a scare tactic, it never stuck with me as I knew deep down I just wanted to be a good person, and as I had the right intentions, I felt that surely God couldn't come after me. Looking back, my parents would step foot in temples — or *mandirs* — light candles, and speak about God. But they themselves were not true believers of what Hinduism represents. It's sad really, as many abusers will use religion as a cover-up for their behaviour. My viewpoint now, as a Hindu, and on celebrating occasions such as Diwali, is frankly straightforward: I believe in my chosen family, spreading love, celebrating each other, and wishing them a future of abundance and peace. There are no strict rules, there are no sinners or winners, and there are no confusing agendas on a religious day. Take away the control and let everyone just be.

If we are speaking about celebrations, I think it's best we mention Christmas Day too. So yes, we also celebrated Christmas Day, and I really enjoyed the idea of Christmas as a child. I actually had some wonderful Christmases, but guess where they were? At my sister's house. I'd enjoy the lead-up to Christmas, as you'd have activities in school. My friends would be excited for Christmas, and the whole city would be covered in decorations and trees being lit up. Back at home, my parents saw Christmas as an *insufferable expense*, so they catered Christmas to their needs instead. No stocking fillers, a small 3ft tree, and one present each under the tree.

Now, please, don't get me wrong, families who go through severe poverty may not even be able to afford that, but we weren't an impoverished household. We had money, quite a fair amount of it actually, but that would only be spent on whatever my mum wanted. So the odd Christmas I got the present I wanted, I felt grateful. Mind you, I put so much emphasis on the types of presents I was getting, because on the actual day, we did nothing as a family. My parents would watch their films, and my brother and I would kill time on his PlayStation. If you look at that wider picture, everyone got to spend Christmas just how they wanted, apart from me. What I wanted was a nice Christmas dinner at the table — laughing, joking, and playing family games all evening. Aside from that neglectful behaviour, on the narc side, my mum would love to start arguments on Christmas Day. The arguments could begin from her not being well, so she's already woken up in a foul mood. That meant all the focus of Christmas Day shifted onto her, because that's how she wanted it. I would seriously put narcissistic people under the statement, "There's no such thing as bad publicity", as they honestly don't care how they seek attention, as long as the focus is on them, that's all that matters.

One particular Christmas, it was bad. Real bad. I had a boyfriend at the time, and he brought me some lovely presents, including a designer watch. My brother was also dating his now-to-be wife at the time, and he was opening up his presents from her. My mum was sat silently observing our behaviour around opening the gifts, and because we were ecstatic that we had been gifted nice things from our partners, my mum began raging in jealousy. However, as we know with narcs, they can't admit their wrongs. So even though I could tell from her eyes that she was seeing green, she spun the narrative that I shouldn't be *showing off* the gifts I got from my boyfriend — because, at the time, my brother's girlfriend "isn't meant to know" that I'm dating someone, as my "name" would look bad in the family.

Anyone reading this part of my story must think this sounds ridiculous, but this was the sad reality of my situation. My brother and I argued against her, disputing why things should be a secret from one another when we are all grown adults. She hated that. She couldn't stand that we didn't just obey her like we were some muppets. The arguing would escalate, and our dad would get involved and shout the loudest, hoping we'd shut up, but that didn't work. I couldn't believe that on a special family day like Christmas, my mum wanted to cause trouble because of her jealousy and that she could never see her children happy. That always disgusted me about her. So then my brother and I went, got dressed, and jumped in his car as soon as we could to drive to my sister's house, and we called her on the way to explain the situation. Yet again, my sister is in a position to put her needs aside to offer support to her siblings. Once we arrived at my sister's house, my brother and I were deflated by our parents' behaviour. We sat and explained everything to my sister and brother-in-law whilst their children played around their Christmas tree — and we felt safe, heard, and protected. My brother-in-law made the decision that he wasn't going to let the parents come over this Christmas, as he had had enough of their behaviour. He didn't want his own family's Christmas ruined, and I totally understood this. The original plan was that we would have all come over as a family and then after the Christmas dinner (which my dad would eat even though he wouldn't dare to suggest making a Christmas dinner himself with fear of retribution from his wife) the parents would leave as they always wanted to get home early, whereas me and my brother just like anyone else wanted to spend the whole day celebrating, joyfully. Hours had passed, and there was no sign of our parents. So we assumed they must have felt shame and knew it wouldn't be wise to show their faces at the house. But as I stated before, for a pair of narcs, "There is no such thing as bad publicity". And behold, they were at the door. They turned up in the early evening. My sister let them in only on the basis that they had presents for the children. So they entered, and within an hour, my brother-in-law could feel the intense tension that had built up and how upset I was over what had happened in the home in the morning. My brother-in-law decided to question them as he didn't want to play the *fake family* card today, and my sister supported him on this. In the typical fashion of my parents, my mum started lying through her teeth, saying that whatever my brother and I said to them was false. That it never happened, and we overreacted. They took no accountability or apologised for causing chaos on Christmas morning. So my brother-in-law said it was best they leave his home immediately, as he didn't want the rest of the day ruined by a pair of liars. As my mum started her victim tears, my dad enabled her behaviour and began squaring up to my brother-in-law. We knew this wouldn't end well. My brother-in-law ended up having to tell them to leave the house. I remember, as they walked back to their car, I was shouting at them with so much anger and disappointment. Telling them that I never wanted to see them again, that they ruined everything, and that I was disgusted by their behaviour. There must have been much more, but this was many years ago — when I was in my early 20s — so I can only remember snippets. I do remember my brother and sister having to hold me back in the doorway to calm me down and bring me back in the house to salvage any last bit of Christmas day we had left.

Over time, these sorts of experiences with abusers can leave you feeling hopeless, confused, and deflated. The hardest part is when you are in a family dynamic with them, and this can make it so much harder to leave. You feel you are breaking away from everything you've ever known, or what everyone else in the world has. But once you rip that band-aid off for good, you realise not everyone comes from a *perfect* family, and you truly aren't alone. In fact, the world is such a big place. There are many people you will meet who have very troubled backgrounds, with whom you can find some relation.

I think it might be wise, if I'm speaking about celebrations, to mention the first year I went no contact, and what I truly celebrated within that year. I didn't understand a celebration until then.

I moved into my apartment, all on my own. That is to be celebrated. I turned 30 and had the most peaceful, joyous birthday celebrations — not just one round of celebrations, but two. I ended the year with the continuous no-contact rule, and I felt good about it. Really good, in fact. I never wanted to look back. These were celebrations I could claim all on my own — with no one lingering to ruin it, no one hiding behind a shadow waiting to come out and hurt me or disappoint me, and no one stopping me from celebrating as loudly or as quietly as I pleased.

6

I'M ONLY ON THIS EARTH TO HELP

From a very young age, my mum made it clear to me that I was only born to *help*, and what she meant by that was to help her and the rest of the family. But not in a way you'd think, more in a way of being able to cater to whatever needs she had. Most girls are born into families and are called *princesses*, but that wasn't the narrative for me; I was indeed only there to help and be used when it suited my parents' needs. As I've mentioned previously, most of the time, they neglected me because they didn't want me to be seen or heard, and found my presence an inconvenience to them. So they'd rather put me somewhere they didn't need to take any responsibility. It's sad because most of my life, I tried to escape that household — by not being in it and moving away at any chance I could — but I always had to return. And because I didn't get married young like both my siblings, I ended up living with the abusers for probably the longest time.

When I was young, I was always called upon to help with the family. I had to learn things from a very young age, but my brother got away with actually being the *princess*, and his needs were met most of the time. I was the only one who was happy to help when I was young, because I got validation from my parents, which is something I associated with being good and being loved.

As I got older and reached the final stages of living with my parents, they were ageing too. I mentioned earlier in the book that they had major surgeries shortly before I decided to go no contact, but in this chapter, I want to go into more detail.

I want to explain how a narc parent will use their illness for several different reasons. Firstly, they would use it as a defence mechanism. If someone went against them, my mum would suddenly claim she'd had a flare-up of her arthritis and that it was all our fault. So, she'd go from angrily shouting at us to crying and asking for sympathy. Any human who has empathy at a young age will immediately feel that they may need to stop and see if she needs help. The next is for financial gain. My parents both played the *disability card*. They had the benefits of a disability car, disability badge for parking, and other financial perks.

One evening, I could hear arguing from my bedroom, and I knew it was them. The murmurs were getting louder and more threatening, so I couldn't sleep — and believe me, I spent as long as I could in my bed to avoid having to deal with them. But they just wouldn't stop. So I got up and went to check in on them. My mum was hysterically crying and shouting at my dad at the same time. My dad, partially deaf in one ear, hadn't worn his hearing aid to sleep — so he was grunting to her that he had no idea what she was talking about. If I look back, it's like two toddlers having a tantrum with each other. I asked what was going on, and she explained that she needed the bedside tool for assistance to get in and out of bed — but it had been stored in the attic by my worthless father. I speak with as little emotion as possible — calm and collected was always my go-to tactic to try my best to get the situation over and done with. I said that neither Dad nor I were capable of going into the attic, seeing as it's 3 am and we're all exhausted. I mentioned that we could figure out another way or give her assistance. This did *not* go down well with her at all — and she screamed, whilst crying at the same time, that she needed that bedside tool NOW. There was never any reasoning with this woman. I was getting frustrated, as I knew she wasn't going to give up — but I was conscious that I had to wake up for work in the next few hours. And going up to that attic felt like a complete waste of time. If she knew she needed this tool after her surgery, why didn't they prepare in advance and get this sorted beforehand? As expected, my dad caved once his hearing aid was back in — and asked me to get the bedside tool from the attic, as he was unable to. The staircase that pulls out was broken, and it almost needed a more flexible, smaller person to jump up and into the attic using mainly core strength. This is what I proceeded to do — through gritted teeth. Once the bedside tool was out of the attic and in the bedroom, I immediately left them to sort it out on the bed. I was pissed off that now I was wide awake and wouldn't be able to settle straight-away to sleep.

As I went back to my bedroom, I heard my mum shout, "She's a selfish bitch, and look at the face she had on her while handing us the bedside tool".

I wanted to explode with anger when I heard that, because she was projecting her own personality at that point. If nobody had gone into that attic, she would have never got what she asked for. Once again, a narc parent will show you, time and time again, that you are not good enough for them. No one is good enough for them.

My Mind - Yebba

Despite all of this, I've helped them go to countless hospital appointments, fetched their medications from the pharmacy after I'd finished work, assisted them with reading doctors' letters, helped my dad organise his insulin pens, helped set up their helpline emergency pendants, and quite a bit more. The reason I list all of these things is to show that I was conditioned to help, and I never had a choice. I wasn't treated with an inch of respect and felt deflated each and every time I tried to *help*. I felt exhausted — mentally and physically — and while all this was going on, in between their hospital visits for various problems, my brother and his wife felt the need to take over and butt into things that frankly didn't concern them at the time (especially not his wife). The pressure was so overwhelming for me. I was barely eating — I looked like a shadow of myself in the mirror. Colleagues at work were concerned, and others around me pointed out the same, but I couldn't tell anyone what was happening. The history was too long to explain why they were behaving the way they were now, and I knew no one was going to do anything about it.

I have transformed the way I help now. I have been so focused on my own healing journey that I've prioritised myself and will do whatever it takes to help myself first.

They say you can't pour from an empty cup and that is damn right. I take time out for myself now, rest when I need to, be productive when I need to, and focus on what feels good and right for me. This has led me to sort a lot of things out that needed some TLC in my life, whereas before, I just didn't have time. It helps that I don't have people around me who drain me of the ability to be supportive or help, and I've found a passion for helping people through my advocacy.

My advocacy has only just started, but any vulnerable person who reaches out to me and feels I've been able to help them, whether that be through advice or simply just to listen, makes me feel fulfilled and that I am aligning with my life's purpose.

The conditioning of a person is a sad thing to see because if I had decided to let my mum feed into my mind that *I'm only here to help*, I would have surely developed a complex that only surrendering and compromising would give me validation. It could have led to me only feeling good if I *helped* someone, so they were teaching me to base my self-worth on the opinion of another person. She'd have made me a people pleaser. If I'd let her condition me the way she wanted, she would have gotten the best of me in her old age — and thank god that never happened.

7

EMPTY THREATS

The reason I've titled this chapter *Empty Threats* is because there was one in particular that was always brought up, yet never acted on: my mum's constant threat that she wanted to commit suicide. She would use this statement every time, when, in her delusional mind, things were "getting out of hand". But what was really happening was that people were waking up to her abusive behaviour and no longer wanted to tolerate it. Therefore, she was losing control. A narc's worst fear.

I want to go back to a memory from when I must have been in my early teens, and an argument had gotten out of hand — it was between both of my parents. I don't recall exactly what happened, but I know it had been pinned on my dad. It seemed to be his fault, and he reacted as my mum hammered him with insults, screaming and shouting in his face. The reaction she got back from him caused her to erupt even further, and this is where both of them would completely lose all sense of dignity and moral ground with each other. By this point, objects would be thrown around the living room, and many swear words and rage would come from them both. But this level of arguing scared the hell out of me. My adrenaline would be through the roof, and I'd feel like I needed to go and diffuse the situation — a very common theme in that home.

As I approached my parents and told them they needed to calm down and just listen to each other, it seemed to make things worse. My mum ran up the stairs and locked herself in the main bedroom. (The reason we had locks on that door was because my parents stored gold in that room, and we had already experienced a robbery in the house.) However, I realise now, as an adult, that the lock was in fact another tool for my mum's manipulation. When she locked herself in the bedroom, my dad, brother and I decided to keep quiet in the house, assuming this was her way of asking for space. Unfortunately, the silence was eerie — and short-lived. Not long after she was in the bedroom, my dad went up to check on her. She began screaming through the door, cussing him out even more for now trying to apologise, saying, "You are the one who caused this trouble in the first place". So here we go. Back to square one. There was nothing my brother or I could do to calm her down. After a while of back-and-forth screaming and shouting, she supposedly decided she didn't want to live this life and told us she was going to take all her medication in the form of pills and kill herself.

At such a young age, my heart was palpitating — because even though my mum was a deeply disturbed person, I still had blind care for her. She was my mum. I pleaded with my dad that we couldn't let this happen, and so did my brother. Eventually, the house fell eerily silent again. We kept asking her to respond, and when she didn't, I genuinely thought that evening she had left us. We went back downstairs and devised a plan for my dad to kick the door down. After a moment of collecting his thoughts, that's exactly what he did. He kicked the door down so the lock was free, and what I saw was the most tragic thing in my entire life.

He found my mum on the bed, on her phone. I felt like a complete fool. I couldn't believe that only 20 minutes ago she was threatening to kill herself — and by not opening the door, we all genuinely believed she may have actually done it. But to find her on the phone, as if nothing had happened, was a complete mockery of my feelings. It made me question everything I had seen that evening.

At the time, I didn't know the term for narcissistic, but I knew *crazy*, and crazy was definitely the word I had for her.

An empty threat makes you feel like you're on the edge of your seat. It makes you feel like you're walking a tightrope and could fall at any minute — but you don't. It makes you feel like you're so close to a fire that it could burn you if you lean in any closer. And it makes you doubt what is to be scared of, and what isn't. This is why I feel that this type of emotional blackmail is so damaging — because you don't know whether to believe what's about to happen or not, and your own safety gauge becomes compromised. And that can lead you into some dangerous situations.

Fast forward to when I was going through the process of cutting contact, I found some evidence. A text message from my mum saying that if I didn't listen to the demands she and my dad had made, and if I returned home, they would be "fast asleep due to all the pills they'd taken". It was yet another empty threat. But this time, I was fully aware of what it was. I never returned home, and I didn't care what they did. They didn't need saving — just like that phone call she once took, the fake attempt was soon forgotten.

8

COMPARISON

Looking back over the past few chapters, you might be thinking one of two things. The first: *This is hard to comprehend.* The second: *I understand — because I've lived something similar.* Let's unpack both of those thoughts in this next chapter.

The *I can't comprehend your abuse* is the thought of someone who hasn't experienced emotional trauma at the hands of a narcissist. They haven't had to walk on eggshells, feel lost and confused about where they stand in that relationship or had to literally remind themselves each day that it's not their fault, it's the narcissist's. Let's try and paint a picture of what Sonam's life would have looked like if she were the type of girl who could read this story in another book and say, "Wow, I can't comprehend this. Why would a parent do this? Is this even real?"

That Sonam would have been brought up by the same set of parents, both born in Africa, who then moved over to the UK after an arranged marriage. She would witness her parents' hardships as they struggled with identifying as

British Indians in a predominantly white country. They would struggle to find jobs that would pay their way in the country so they can have a stable life. The struggle would also be felt in the marriage, as it was two people who married young under the expectations of their Indian parents, but really they weren't too sure if this was what they wanted and hadn't formed a true identity outside of their lives in Africa.

These would be the true struggles that this alternative Sonam could see. She'd feel empathy for them, but she also experienced the immense love from her hardworking parents. She would witness her dad go to work every single day so he could provide the necessities for his wife to make delicious home-cooked meals each evening. The mum would make them without hesitation as she'd never dream of seeing her daughter go hungry. When the family spent time together in the evenings, it was full of laughter and sharing details about their day. The mum would wish to educate herself and promised she would get a form of education so she could also provide and be an inspiring influence in her daughter's life. When her daughter came home from school, the mum would ask her how her day was, and attentively listen as Sonam yaps on about her day from start to finish.

The mum would then make sure dinner was ready and shortly after, she'd want to make sure that Sonam certainly wasn't left alone all evening in her room. No, she would make sure she'd read to Sonam before bed, a peaceful, tranquil bedtime story that would help her daughter sleep, tucked in with a kiss on the forehead. Sonam's dad would be present, oh, he would be very present in his daughter's life. On the weekend he would make sure the car was full of snacks and drinks and off they all went on a family road trip. It might be to go visit an English town that they'd never seen, so the dad could gain his confidence and expand his awareness of the country he lived in. Sonam would be in the back seat of that silver Mercedes, and she would laugh, sing, and smile as they passed along beautiful countryside roads. She felt safe around her dad, like he could solve any problem in the whole wide world. This Sonam never needed much—she just wanted a set of parents who, even with their own worries and problems, created a home that felt like solace. A place where we could all rest our heads and look at one another with contentment, knowing: this is home, and nothing bad can happen here. This Sonam has the continued support of her parents. As she gets older, she reflects back on her childhood memories with love and respect for her parents, knowing that they did whatever it took to get it right for their children. Sonam would acknowledge that no one is perfect, but she would still admire all the little quirks that her parents had. Sonam would be proud of her mum as she followed through on that education and became an English teacher later in life, and she would respect her dad as he took on various jobs, then finally opened up his business later in life too. Sonam would reflect back on her family's achievements and would have pursued her dream job too, with the help and encouragement from both of her parents. Sonam would pass through life with ease, confidence, respect, self-love love and a quiet humbleness which most people found quite endearing. One day, Sonam would walk into a bookstore and pick up this story and feel a deep sense of sympathy for the other girl called Sonam.

Another Sonam would grow up feeling alone, abandoned and lost in the world. The people she wanted so badly just to love her in this life have truly let her down. This Sonam could unfortunately still be living in a toxic family system, or she's planning her way out, but both scenarios mean she is still hurting and in pain. When the abuse starts is a question that racks through her brain on a daily basis, because the majority of narcissistic abuse is invisible. The fact that this Sonam is questioning this means she needs help. This Sonam was always in fight or flight mode, and to a point, she didn't understand why. The lack of information or vocal speakers on this type of abuse meant that Sonam normalised the pain.

Sonam normalised feeling depressed, at her lowest points, the nights spent crying silently in her room alone. She had normalised going to school and fantasised about having her friends' parents. She normalised her dad's aggression and each night tried to calm her parents down after they had a fight. She normalised seeing her mum be fake in-front of her, giving the odd compliment because she knew her friends were present, but Sonam knew just from the tone of voice and facial expression her mum gave that she never meant any of the compliments, it was just so she could be looked at as a wonderful mother. This Sonam normalised the siblings always being on and off with each other, she normalised trying to change her selfish brother. This Sonam normalised way too much, until one day she would walk into the bookstore, pick up this story, and think, *oh my god, this author had the same life as me. I totally understand her pain.*

Since I began posting on the social media platform called TikTok, I've really had a mixed bag of opinions. The classic,

"But there are two sides to the story", always comes up. This is for a number of reasons, but the main ones are that they don't see physical damage, there was no sexual assault, so as people can't see the physical damage, they don't believe mental abuse happens, so then they will want to hear my parents' side of the story. There are many people out there who aren't informed of narcissistic abuse, and don't understand what emotional abuse can feel and look like. Just because I didn't carry any bruises or scars from my abuse, it didn't mean that I didn't have other physical signs. All these things do add up to someone who is experiencing emotional turmoil, as the body has to store and release the pain somehow. Please read *The Body Keeps the Score* by Bessel Van De Kolk, and this will keep you well informed of how the body reacts to trauma. The effect it has on your mind is that you are constantly reliving the traumatic events that happened. You are rehearing all the abusive comments and trying to rewire your brain to not believe those comments, you are having to pick yourself up and go to work on a day where you've had next to nothing of sleep and your brain has become frazzled with all the abusive energy and arguments you've had to deal with the night before. Your brain is anxious, paranoid and wondering what your next step is so you don't have to face more trauma.

Another point to add to this comment is that there can never be two sides to the story when abuse starts from childhood. One thing to remember is that I was a child when the abuse started, so there was no way that I would have caused it, aggravated it, or encouraged the abuse. But when I post online, people don't see my younger self; they don't see a child, so they automatically judge that I would have been a rude, selfish daughter who wanted attention and is disrespectful to my parents. I speak candidly online and have said I'd welcome it if my parents ever posted online, but I know they wouldn't. One key thing about narcs is that once they are exposed, there is no going back for them, and it means that many people will begin to see the facade behind the mask.

The positive messages have been to do with my bravery, strength and how eloquently I speak in my videos. Sometimes I'm not sure how to receive this, as it took so many years to recognise the abuse I was going through and to find my voice was very difficult. I guess the only thing that kept me going was the fact that I've always appreciated expression, expression of the self was so intrinsically linked to who I am as a person, my outlet was writing. I began my writing from as young as I can remember, and the words landing on the page felt like I had a voice. It felt like my mouth wasn't taped shut and that I could freely express what was going on in my own mind, and what I was processing and coming to terms with. I even began writing a fantasy novel at the age of either 15 or 16, and it was my life, but in a different form. I was trying to express what was happening in my household, but needed to create a new character, otherwise having the actualisation that this was my real life would have surely sent me into a downward spiral into nothingness. So I wrote and continued this on and off for years. Until I, at around the age of 29 or so, accepted that this is a key part of who I am. I love books, I love to read and most importantly to write, and because of this, you are sitting here today reading my story.

Tortured poet

9

THE THINGS WE TELL OURSELVES

The things we tell ourselves are so important. It's important to sit with yourself, alone, to figure out the noise in your head. No distractions, no phones, no people, and certainly no time limit.

I'll begin to share my life after trauma, or even living with trauma in the present day, but first, we will reflect back to when I was a child again. Even though, as a child, I was left alone a lot — and this caused me to have an anxious attachment style with relationships growing up — I was always worried that the person I loved was going to abandon me, because this had already happened to me since birth. The abandonment wound would scare off potential partners, and then my next fear would turn into a reality — and that was feeling like a burden. Past relationships, even if they did love me, struggled with my *need* for love. It's like I was a well without any water, and no matter how many times someone tried to fill it up, it ran dry.

Once I sought out therapy and began my spiritual awakening in my mid-20s, I realised the things I was telling myself — well, most of them were false — but I was conditioned to believe them:

- *No one will ever want me, or love me.*
- *If I love this person correctly, the way they want, then I'll get the love I need back.*
- *I crave affection, so I'll ask for it. But when I get it, it'll never be enough, so I will keep pushing.*
- *If I'm successful, then someone will notice me.*

Some of these ideals got stuck in my head, along with multiple other low self-esteem thoughts. As my mind was on that frequency for a lot of my life, I was attracting the wrong people and partners. I was crushing my soul as each year passed, not understanding that on top of the nasty comments my mum would say to me, I was adding to those negative thoughts through the people surrounding me. I started learning to rewire my perspective of myself and decided to say more of the below:

- *I am deserving of love, so if someone wants to love me, I will let them without question.*
- *I am wanted and needed in this world, as I have a purpose greater than my being.*
- *I have learnt healthier ways of expressing love to someone, and if that is not enough for them, then I know my worth to leave.*
- *The affection I like is good for me as it releases positive endorphins throughout my body, but I am capable of self-soothing, too.*
- *I will not put my all into being successful, as the only person I would need to impress is myself.*

See how already, if you're reading this, the impact it makes on our mind when we speak positive affirmations to it. What other people say to us we can't control, unfortunately. But on the flip side, we can't absorb what people say to us. And believe it or not — this might sound controversial — but even the good things, don't absorb them too much. The purpose behind this is simple: if you let other people consume you, you'll never have any self-perception or opinion about yourself. This is where sitting alone, having time out, comes into play. When victims are going through narc abuse, the abuser will never let you have a minute to yourself — whether they're in their rage or not. To them, you're a puppet that's dangled in front of them and should be available at any given moment to be used if needed. The narc will cloud your own judgement and not let you think.

I remember the days living in that house — the shouting was non-stop, continuous all evening and night. Even if I was isolated in my room, my mum was so violently loud I could hear her all the way from downstairs. How that woman never exhausted herself from all that anger and shouting, I'll never know.

Once I cut out and came away from that situation, space and being alone was all that I wanted. Actually, it was needed. I could collect my thoughts in a safe space and talk myself out of any negative, belittling thoughts I had. Any thought or memory that was hazy became clearer, so I could process what I witnessed and affirm that my feelings are valid.

I never understood the importance of solitude, and when I began living alone, this became clear to me. If you had told little Sonam that one day she'd live alone, she would never have pictured it — or accepted it — as the thought would have scared the hell out of her. However, the solitude meant I could connect with myself on a deeper level. I could provide comfort and security, and I enjoyed the privacy of my own thoughts. With solitude can come peace, and I finally found that peace. The peace within my soul. Once I got rid of the poison, I could flourish.

Now my next challenge was to have this mindset in a relationship, and I'm proud to say I accomplished this. I was able to be in a healthy partnership without the need to depend or rely. I could freely love and be loved without any agendas or motives. Yes, did my childhood wounds sometimes show up? Of course they did. That's because trauma never leaves you — you just have to learn how to manage it. But when those wounds came, I saw it as a learning opportunity to know myself better. I can now have my partner, but still cherish the times when I'm alone to sit with my thoughts.

I want to talk about the PTSD I've endured so far on my healing journey. I never used to have nightmares about my toxic family when they were in my life — I only began having them after I left. Now, if you look into this deeper, it just shows that my nightmare was my living reality — it just hadn't fully hit my subconscious what was happening. My life after trauma is so peaceful and calm that these nightmares only haunt me when I sleep — but they're teaching me things. They're teaching me that there's deeper healing that needs to be done, and we've only touched the surface. They're telling me this is what happened to me, and showing me the intensity of the pain I endured. I hate to say it, but sometimes we need to remind ourselves of this pain to make sure we don't walk back into the fire.

The PTSD can show up in other ways — in triggers when I'm out and about, meeting new people, or facing certain situations. The key to PTSD is that the flashbacks can be horrendous, but the healing that comes from unpacking them is important. It's crucial to understanding your soul better.

They say timing is everything in this life. Sometimes I wonder — did I need to face all those years of suffering, living in silence, and covering up my pain just to now reach freedom?

The timing of going no contact couldn't have happened at a better time — even though, if I could've taken a magic wand and left the family home at 16, I would have. But I didn't have that magic wand. Some will argue why it took me so long to leave my toxic family. It's because, as I said before, the timing couldn't have been better for when I did. My sister and I had to take that leap together — side by side, and at that time, literally living under the same roof. I know my sister has her own story to tell. And even though she's 20 years older, I know she has her regrets about not leaving sooner. But that's her story to live through and share. What we have to recognise is when the universe did work out in our favour — and why it did. It needed our collective energy, our collective mindset, to overcome this hurdle of cutting your parents out of your life for good. Enough that you won't even be present at their funeral.

I am immensely proud of me and my sister for this new direction in life. I remember a conversation — sat in my sister's living room with my brother-in-law — where we talked about the potential betrayal we might face from one another. How heartbreaking is that, really? When all you've ever known is your *loved ones* turning their back on you, you start to question even your real loved ones when your whole family system comes crashing down. My sister was scared that one day, in my loneliness, I might suddenly forget everything that's happened in my life and reach for my phone — unblock my mum and speak with her. She was paranoid that our parents would rear their ugly heads back into my life and take me away from her — leaving her with no one. I was scared that my sister was tired of living through the same battle she'd had with our mum since she was a young girl — and I worried that she'd be too drained to keep going with no contact, that she might give in. I was worried she might be tempted to know what our mum was saying about her behind her back, and that she'd open up that dialogue again. The fear was real. We had to speak openly and honestly with each other about these different scenarios, just to calm each other's nerves — to reassure ourselves that this would never become a reality. And it didn't.

In my mind, there was never a way back to my toxic parents. That bridge was burnt — and there's no one around to help build it again. I didn't want it to be built again. But I can empathise with people who struggle with that battle in their minds. Some people do go back to their toxic family members, even after managing to leave the system for a few years or so. For me, because I created my own little family — consisting of only a handful of people — that's all I needed. I created a home within myself.

The discoveries you make once going no contact are huge, and these self-discoveries may last for years to come. Unfortunately, when you're being abused or living in trauma, it's so deep-rooted in your daily life, your habits, and the way you view the world that it takes a lot of work to unlearn all of those behaviours. As I grew up in quite a neglectful household, I learned some bad habits. One of those habits was around food. As my mum began avoiding cooking for us after a certain age, we had to learn how to make quick, easy meals — and I didn't want to spend too much time in the kitchen, because I knew I'd be walking on eggshells with my mum there. I just didn't have the ability to handle all of that at once. I remember eating pasta with tomato ketchup and grated cheese for dinner, time after time. It weirdly became a comfort food of mine — it was reliable, did the job, and was stress-free to make. I did it just so I wouldn't go hungry. That's another form of survival mode. I realised that in that house, I was avoiding my parents at all costs — and I became self-reliant. I couldn't deal with spending any time with them, because 9 times out of 10 it would turn into a malicious argument, or I'd end up feeling broken from all the gaslighting.

Another thing is gaslighting, which is when someone doesn't remember it happening or being said that way. This can be extremely dangerous to a victim because they question their own reality. Imagine someone is constantly telling you that your thought or memory of something is wrong — imagine how that would make you feel? You know in your mind that whatever has been said or done is the truth, but someone who is gaslighting you will flip this around and try to erase it all. You will get to a point of bowing down to the gaslighter, as you feel powerless, helpless, and not hopeful that they are seeing things the way you are. This is why I tried to avoid my parents at all costs, because my mum would always say, "That never happened". This is why I had to take my evidence, this is why I needed the facts —

because that woman was determined to change the narrative every single time. I hate to admit it, but because of my trauma, I do feel that my memory isn't the sharpest it could be, and that hasn't improved even after going no contact. Thankfully, I don't have anyone around me who is trying to gaslight me or change my reality in life anymore.

Another habit I picked up — again, because of survival mode — was to avoid confrontation. Now, I still to this day won't want confrontation if I can help it, because the feeling of shouting, aggression, purposely saying nasty comments to hurt one another, doors or things being slammed — it seriously takes me back to a dark place. I've learnt how to lean into the balance of communicating with boundaries with people, so that it doesn't escalate into a full-blown argument. I've also learnt how to communicate openly and honestly if I feel there's something on my mind or that a boundary has been crossed. Don't get me wrong — I'm only human and can still get pissed off, but that can be resolved. Prior to this, my habit of not wanting confrontation meant that I would lose my voice. I'd get so upset, I'd instantly start to cry and couldn't handle it all. Because of this, the other person would then view me as weak — someone who would crumble if something was discussed. I had to learn how to hold my own when it came to someone who was argumentative.

After going no contact, something I realised was that no matter what happens in my life, the sun sets and rises just the same. I've had successes and downfalls during this time, and it's crossed my mind during both — *wouldn't it be nice to have a parent to speak to about this, or lean on?* But I had to learn how to stand on my own two feet — that no one is going to comfort me more than me, and no one is going to clap louder for me than me. This might seem sad to some, but this is the reality when you have to cut away from family. Your problems become your own, and you have to focus on taking it day by day with whatever situation life throws at you. To my loved ones — you know who you are — who have stood by me during these turbulent times, I will always value you.

No one teaches you any of this — that the habits you create from a toxic environment can impact your daily life or health. I know there were a few more habits I'd picked up, but as I'm on track to unlearn all of those behaviours, it can feel like a past version of myself that I don't resonate with anymore.

I now want you to pause and take a second to think about any bad habits you may have taken on from being in a toxic environment.

If your mind came up with some habits, that's okay. The whole process of healing from trauma — unlearning and learning behaviours — is that no one becomes perfect from this. No amount of learning or healing will erase the trauma from my memories, and that's not what self-growth is about. Self-growth is growing further from the pain, being dedicated to ensuring that you don't live that same life of pain anymore. It's about empowering yourself again.

Tom Odell - Heal

10

AM I A NARCISSIST?

In my last chapter, I spoke about how important it is to speak positive affirmations to yourself, because the things we say to ourselves can make a huge impact on our lives. As I began to dig deep into the world of narcissistic abuse, I found myself questioning — *could I ever be a Narc?* This scared the hell out of me, as I'd spent my entire life up until this point trying to be the opposite of both of my parents. I was never inspired by my mum and had disregarded my dad. So when I realised you can get narcissists in different forms, I began to wonder — *have any of these traits ever been me?*

Let me get one thing clear — if anyone questions whether they're a narc, there's the highest chance that they're not one. The self-reflection, self-devotion, and self-awareness it takes to even know what a narc is — and then to look inward first, making sure you aren't one before calling someone else out — that's a high form of emotional intelligence. You're making sure you're not causing pain, hurt, or emotional damage to the people around you — loved ones or even strangers — and that's also a quality of a highly empathic person. Let's say you did feel you had narc tendencies. If you're prepared to work on those and change your ways for the better, then you most likely didn't have narc tendencies to begin with — just some very human flaws.

I reflect back in depth on all the people who have crossed paths with me — this could be friends, ex-partners, and family members. I can say, hand on heart, that any person who's entered my life and had to leave it, there was always a reason. And I've not had anyone openly express to me that they've been cruelly hurt by any of my actions. I'm taking this as a good sign — because in these past relationships, at some point I've always tried to put myself in their shoes and see things from their perspective before jumping the gun and coming in all guns blazing. It shows the amount of consideration I have for others. I can put these relationships or friendships not working out down to the fact that we were different people, and it just wasn't meant to be.

The funny thing about children who grow up in a narcissistic household is that we're always trying to promote the good. Many of us, even with trust issues, still believe that good people can exist out in the world. We believe that one day we can be loved and can love, and we cherish the good things in life. We don't want to involve ourselves with negativity, gossip, or drama — and will avoid, at all costs, anyone who brings us pain. This is mainly true for those who have begun healing on their journey. I do understand, however, that some will repeat the same patterns over and over and can't break the cycle of abuse. This is what makes things funny — that once you cut away from toxic family, people are so quick to judge and throw out comments like, "It's shameful to speak about your parents that way" or "You only get one mum". But what they fail to realise is that you're just trying to live a happy life. No attention needed. No sympathy even. You just want to be free, in your own mind and your own life. Tell me, what's so shameful about that? Remember — if you're calling out abuse or any wrongdoing, regardless of who it is, you are fighting the good fight.

Back to narcissistic behaviour. Once I realised, quite quickly, that I wasn't a narc, my attention turned to other people in my close circle. I realised that if I ever encountered a narc again, I'd be calling out their bullshit straight away and making a swift exit. There was no chance in hell, if I had any say, that I'd be surrounding myself with that behaviour. So my *narc radar*, as I like to call it, was on — and it would be scanning everyone I met. The main spotlight was on men I might have a relationship with. I'm not too proud to admit that two of my past partners displayed signs of being a narc. They were entitled, selfish, and would only show me love or affection if they could use it against me. They were belittling, dishonest, cheated, and tried to subtly force control over me. They never took any accountability and were only concerned about how I made them feel. I can say, in short — this radar came damn in handy when I started dating again. And it's safe to say, I didn't attract any more narc partners. Now, when it came to friendships, that's always a bit trickier — you're not with them all the time and can't always observe their personality in different situations. The only thing I can say about friendships is that usually, a narc person will stand out in a group setting — they'll be quick to take control, make the conversation all about them, and treat the friendship as transactional. If they benefit from the friendship, you'll see more of them around. I have a few close friends in my life, but I've learnt — everyone has to come with a boundary.

11

EXTENDED FAMILY ALIENATION

The biggest surprises come when you go no contact, and when you've exposed your family to the world. My dad's side of the family was always a topic we couldn't speak about at home, as our mum had created the narrative that my dad's mother, four sisters, and brother were all abusive to her when she first got married into that family. Unfortunately, when you're young and naive, you believe this — and we did believe it, wholeheartedly. That she was abused. That she was treated badly by her in-laws. My dad made the narrative more believable, as he would be apologetic to her whenever she kicked off at him about her *past traumas*. On reflection though, it was complete attention-seeking. Her outbursts would come from nowhere, and she'd blame my dad for a number of things that supposedly went wrong in the past with his family. He would usually act confused and then apologise. And then the cycle would repeat. Over and over again. No one ever sat us down and had a mature conversation to let us know what actually happened.

The alienation got stranger as time went on. I remember, out of the blue, my parents were hosting a religious ceremony at the house involving a priest — apparently it was in respect to my grandfather, who I never met. He was the only person my mum ever spoke kind words about. Mind you, this ceremony took place many years after he actually passed, so at the time, I was unsure what my mum's true intentions were. Even though she made out that she hated these people, she invited every single one of them to the ceremony. With my knowledge now, this is a very typical narc move — so she could look like the best person in the family, like she was willing to forgive her *abusers*. When the extended family came, they only came for my grandfather — and I believe they possibly wanted to make amends with my dad, not necessarily his wife. My mum accepted gifts from these guests, hosted the ceremony, and made sure that me, my brother, and my sister all played our *characters* for the day. Now, my memory is a bit hazy, but it was either around this time, or just after, that I was able to reconnect with my cousins for a short while. I even went to Disneyland Paris with them.

I remember at the time, I felt quite good — it was nice to have other girls around my age to talk to and hang out with. But once again, something happened, and it was all taken away from me. I wasn't allowed to speak to those cousins, aunts, or my uncle anymore. It went back to how it was before, where we were meant to hate them because of how they'd treated my mum. It felt unfair to me. I couldn't understand how my mum could happily interact with these people, but in the same breath, hate them and want them gone from all of our lives. My sister told me this was a pattern that had happened even when I was little. My mum would try to reconnect with my dad's side of the family, and then almost instantly cut them off again.

Knowing my mum's behaviour now, there are a lot of missing pieces to that puzzle with my dad's side of the family. But more than anything, I remember them not being that keen to connect with her — only with my dad. That shows me they must have seen right through my mum when she married into the family. My mum must have done something to them.

I never really knew my grandmother. She was extremely quiet the few times I saw her, and her energy came across as vacant. She lived until she was quite old, apparently had dementia, and then passed. My grandfather passed a long time ago, and somehow we had a picture of him in our living room at home. I used to look at him — looking a bit like my dad, but a stranger nevertheless.

My mum convinced my dad that they should attend my grandmother's funeral because, being the eldest sibling in that family, my dad was entitled to her inheritance. Mind you, this on-and-off connection with her would've caused a lack of trust, and no strong foundation for her to leave it to him in the first place. They never cared for her in her last days, and now my mum wants her hands on the inheritance. Quite sick really.

I refused to go to the funeral, along with my sister and brother, because we all felt — how could they turn up to the funeral of someone they claimed was *abusive*, someone we had no bond with? And yet, they shamelessly went and witnessed — I can only imagine — people experiencing real grief. Once again, what went through my parents' heads during those moments, I'll never know. But I do know that nothing my parents have ever done has been with pure intentions.

Now, back to that big surprise after going no contact. One of my first cousins reached out to me over social media. She'd seen my story and wanted to share her sympathies with me. I was shocked, but deep down, I'd hoped that someone from our dad's side would reach out. Me and my sister had a string of unanswered questions — ones we knew might not be fully answered by my cousin — but it was time for us to judge people based on our own experiences, not the bullshit that had been fed into our heads by our parents.

Turns out this cousin, who I hadn't seen or spoken to in around 15 years, seemed keen to speak with me. Not just because of our family history, but because she had the same feelings of confusion about what happened in our family. She wanted to connect with me on a deeper level, and it turns out the three of us — me, my sister, and her — ended up meeting.

Maybe when you lose one thing, another returns.

12

BELIEVE PEOPLE WHEN THEY SHOW YOU WHO THEY ARE, THE FIRST TIME

This part of my story was inspired by anger. I had just recently found out that, during my second year of going no contact with my abusive parents, my mum had booked a 3-week trip to Las Vegas with my dad, and they were off at the end of that month. To be clear, I didn't go looking for this news, it came directly to me after a completely different conversation I had with a family member. This is why healing is so messed up. I knew in the first year of cutting them out that my mum had taken a solo trip to Dubai to visit someone, but for some reason, this Las Vegas trip triggered the hell out of me.

To put it in perspective, going no contact — and sticking to it — was a strange harmony of one of the easiest and hardest things I've had to do so far in my life. Each year that goes by, I celebrate the victory of being free from my mum's chains, but I'm also reminded of the loss and grief I've had to face by not having a family. While I struggled with this, my parents are going on holidays. And to me, it felt like they weren't being served their karma. It's a shame, isn't it? As much as I can move forward with my life, the unasked-for abuse I've received from my parents will always be there, like a scar that doesn't fade. I was furious with this information. It reminded me that no matter what they did to us as children, they don't even care. They don't even stop to notice that they've lost two daughters. They don't even notice our absence. And even though I know those people wouldn't, it was still hurting me deep down. It was that stark reminder again that they will both carry on like everything has been fine, when in reality, it wasn't.

The anger took over, and so many mixed emotions came up, just knowing how this type of abuse barely gets any justice. If I were to go into detail about the karma I'd want both of my parents to have really faced, then I'd probably be imprisoned instead — so it's best I don't share.

This incident caused me to think about the word *karma*. It does, in fact, originate from a South Asian and Buddhist background, with the expression: *The sum of a person's actions in this and previous states of existence, viewed as deciding their fate in future experiences.* So let's look at the various angles one could view this statement from:

- *Did I do something in my past life to deserve this karma from my parents?*
- *Did something happen to them in their previous lives, to then become the way they are in this life because of karma?*
- *Will their next lives be hell, because they were devils in this karma?*

So many different ways to look at this, but for someone like me, who's grown to believe that karma is in the hands of the believer, things started to change. And the anger became less over time.

For my parents to suffer their karma, in my opinion, a few things needed to happen to them while they were still alive.

Their reputation had to be shattered. I achieved this when I became vocal about my abuse online, and by, as you're reading now, releasing a book about it.

Their ego had to become deflated. This started happening when friends they'd known for a long time began to accept that they aren't such *good-natured* people, due to the reality of why their daughters walked out of their lives.

They can no longer abuse me anymore, because I removed myself. Now, this was a big one. Without the presence of me or my sister, my mum lost all control, all power, and all knowledge about us. This would have caused her massive frustration because she feeds off others being upset or hurt. Now, if she can't do that to her own homemade dolls, who will she do it to?

Doll House - Melanie Martinez

These are the points I have to remind myself of — that they *will* be experiencing a fraction of karma while they're still alive. As for their next life, who knows? One of my trusted psychics that I visit — let's call him *Tony* — released a book himself a while back, and of course, I purchased it. In that book, he speaks about his spiritual knowledge of karma and goes into detail about how, as souls, we're brought back into the same karma or situations because we haven't learnt the lessons from them, so the cycle continues and continues. So even though there's an innocent person in a bad situation, everyone does have free will and can make a change. If I take that ideology onboard, it means that in this lifetime I had to break the cycle of abuse and leave my parents behind — otherwise, I was in fear of being re-born into the same family, and the same situation, all over again. It's usually the hardest lessons we learn in life that provide the greatest substance.

One thing I want to speak out to the reader is this: abusive parents don't have a conscience, and my experiences with mine prove this. I'm not even a mother, but I couldn't dream of going on luxury holidays knowing that my eldest daughter was in such emotional suffering because of what I'd done to her. Or wondering if my youngest daughter was dead or alive, because the last time I'd seen or heard from her was when she collected bin bags and boxes of her clothes from her bedroom and left. How can someone live with themselves knowing that was the reality? People without a conscience — that's who.

Anger can propel you into some dangerous situations — it can make you reckless, rebellious, and quite frankly, unsafe. That's why I try to harness my power into my writing, vocalising on social media platforms, or leaning heavily into my spiritual practice. Anger is the only emotion that kept my safety senses alive. It knew when I was in danger in that household so I could defend myself. But what good is anger now that I'm living a peaceful life? It will only drain me of my true empathic powers and leave me feeling burnt out. I don't want to be angry at myself. I don't want to look in the mirror and feel angry at the person who's already experienced so much turmoil. Why would I do that? I have to let it go.

So, believe people when they show you who they are the first time. My mum prioritised going on holiday to America and spending money over there — buying clothes, handbags, shoes — but she would always leave us with barely any of that back at home. She was so quick to have a massive, full-blown argument with my dad a week or two before their cruise around Europe. And even after her daughters went no contact, she continued her travels. This shows that this woman has always been the same, and I wish I could've believed it the minute I started understanding things.

13

THE OTHER SIBLING

Up until this point, you've only heard me mention my brother — but now, let's talk about him. In narcissistic families, their allies become their children, but only if you're labelled the golden child. My brother being born, even though it was before me, was both a blessing and a curse. My parents had prayed for him. They literally took a trip to India and prayed to have a son. If you, the reader, are from a South Asian background, you'll get this immediately — that boys are cherished above girls. But even so, parents still expect their daughters to repay the favour in their old age and look after them during ill health. Very unfair, if you ask me. The curse factor was that I grew up thinking my brother would have my back. That he would protect and defend us against the abuse. But once he got married, that changed pretty much everything. I can only suspect, to this day, that my brother and his wife came into the family with an agenda, and that agenda was the inheritance. The reason behind him wanting this inheritance so desperately? I can only pinpoint it to greed.

Does he feel he deserves this after the trauma he witnessed?

Is he just as selfish as his parents, that he feels entitled to all of the inheritance?

Has he picked a partner exactly like our mother — someone with an obsession with money too?

Many unanswered questions, but still important to note. My brother witnessed many things growing up in that abusive household, but he *normalised* it so much that he'd say things like, "But they are still MY parents". Look at the word choice in that statement — not *our* parents, but *my*, meaning only *his*. This goes to show how the abuse put onto children from a young age in a narc family leads to a tactic called *triangulation*, which is where siblings feel they need to compete against each other for their parents' love. They'll do whatever it takes to be front and centre in that parent's eyes, even if it means throwing their own siblings under the bus. Growing up, I hadn't really realised that this was what my brother was doing, whether it was subconscious or not. He would always shapeshift into whatever my parents wanted:

A quiet, reserved boy.

Doesn't cause any trouble.

Doesn't voice his opinions or talk back.

Follows his parents' advice.

Displays sympathy for his elderly parents.

These are all the things my brother did 95% of the time. The other 5% — when he tried to stand his ground or pick the side of his sister — he didn't have the balls, and went back to being quiet again. Not fighting for what was right.

The other sibling can cause a tremendous amount of hurt to the one who needs support, but this isn't common knowledge to everyone. As the reader, you may feel sorry for him. But let me tell you, he only had his own best interests at heart. As the golden child, conditioned by the narcs, he used his selfish behaviour to get what he wanted out of our parents. That may have been a fancy Mercedes, money towards his wedding and the engagement ring for his wife, or my mum slipping him cash in the name of *it's for his kids*. But putting the money aside, he also got more emotional support. The FaceTimes he had with my parents during the COVID-19 lockdown? They spoke to him with pride. Asked him how his day was, how work was going. Took an interest in his wife and kids. Prioritised the call above anything else. The only problem with this emotional support is that it comes with a price. My parents, especially my mum, knew exactly what she was doing with her son. She'd bitch about his wife behind his back — several times — and cause him distress over his own life choices. But as soon as everyone put on a fake smile, all of that got buried.

There was a moment in my life when I lived with my brother. It was temporary — around six months — and I have to say, I felt like a burden. It was awkward living with them. I'd been kicked out again, unfortunately, and this time my brother and sister had to have that conversation about who was going to take me in. I was at breaking point at home, and I didn't care where I went — I just needed somewhere. The decision ended up with me living at my brother's. Evidently, he had more space in his house in the end. Throughout the first few weeks, our mum would bombard his phone with vile, nasty messages, saying he'd failed them as a son, and asking why he was feeding into the narrative that they were, in fact, abusive and bad parents. I knew then that my mum couldn't handle the fact that her precious golden boy was showing some backbone. Unfortunately, it didn't last long. His wife had convinced him, because she lost her dad at a young age, that we should both still be thankful we even had a set of parents. Stupidly, my brother hadn't told his wife the full backstory of the abuse since we were children. He couldn't face his reality. He didn't want to accept that this was the family he was brought up in. So instead, he kept his mouth shut and went along with "let's try and reconcile".

That "let's try and reconcile" led to me and my brother having a really messed up conversation in his living room, where he told me that, even though I was already paying rent while being a student with a minimum wage part-time job, he needed to increase the rent because "toilet roll is expensive". This was a massive insult and a low blow. I was already trying to maintain my dignity by paying rent, and he was expecting more? Because of toilet roll? What level are you trying to compare me to? His visions of his sister were so warped — my disconnect with him started from there.

This disconnect only started getting worse as his wife began to join in. She said she "didn't want to get involved in any drama" — yet here she was, after we went no contact, kissing their ass and doing everything she could with her husband to portray that they weren't in the wrong, and were purely innocent in all of this.

Throughout my life, I hadn't lost my brother just once, but multiple times. I watched him either lose his identity or show his true colours to me because of his narcissistic parents. See, I can do the same as him — they are truly *his* parents. As soon as I went no contact, I disconnected from all of them. He can have them.

14

SURVIVOR

You've read as I've delved deep into my past to unpack the trauma, the memories, and the many challenges I've faced throughout my life. So, where do we go from here? Well, I think we should move to the part of me becoming a survivor.

I think as I started to get older, the neglect I had as a child and as a young teenager turned into independence. The aggression I had to deal with at home meant I became self-resilient and chose to only engage in an argument if it was necessary. The lack of love, support, and affection meant that I created a backbone for myself, and I wasn't afraid of showing love and affection. I was able to cultivate love deep in my stomach and share this with the world, when I'd never experienced an ounce of it from my parents. I started reading people, and reading them very well. I knew that when people started speaking fondly about their parents, I would ask with keen interest, like, "Tell me more about your family?" just to deflect them from asking about mine. Most people fell for this, and would proudly speak about their parents and family. I could see a spark light up in their eyes, and don't get me wrong, it was a nice feeling to see strangers so enthralled by their own family. But it gave me relief from my own shame and embarrassment — the kind I felt even having to speak about my parents. Unfortunately, not everyone was so oblivious. Some would still ask me, "So tell me about your parents?" That's when I learnt to only reveal facts about my parents, never emotions. I rarely post pictures on social media about my parents. Mother's or Father's Day? Well, you can forget about it. I'd just try my best not to look at social media on those days. I feel like, as I learnt to cover quite a lot of things up, many people saw me as quite a private person in certain aspects of my life. When in fact, now that I'm healed, I'm an open book. I can tell people my honest truth without feeling ashamed or embarrassed the way I used to. The shame and embarrassment are not mine to carry. It is the abuser who should carry them.

I learnt how to be a survivor. To survive any situation that was usually thrown at me. Being a survivor is someone who's quite good at not being their most authentic self. It's quite robotic, actually — some would even say a bit cold. I had no other choice, as I was stuck in survival mode and didn't really have an option. This survival instinct, thankfully, didn't lead me down any dangerous paths — which could have easily happened. When you're in survival mode, you're always looking for the next way out, the next exit, or the next time you can feel safe again.

One person I can dedicate this part of the chapter to is my sister. She started off as my sister, but over time, she became a best friend, a fierce protector, a confidant, a supporter, a mother, and a leader. As we got older, we would turn to each other when the waters were really rough at home. The amount of phone calls we had that got us through the evenings, the nights I've spent with her and her family inside their home, the days we shared going out and about, doing the things together that really a mother and daughter should be doing. I could tell, as I got older, that my sister was seeing my personality grow. She could see how I was dealing with the trials and tribulations of the abuse, and she respected how I was handling situations. We started holding each other accountable and making sure neither of us went down the wrong path. We would guide each other through the abuse we'd suffered and fight as a team against any family who tried to tear us down. We'd celebrate each other's wins, and in between, make sure we were having a laugh and enjoying good times together. My sister let me have a bond with her family. Her husband became an inspiration to me — showing me what a great man really is — and a father figure. He didn't have to, but he took me under his wing and gave me a sense of family. My nieces and nephew who I've shared countless memories with as kids — playing, laughing, being mischievous, and caring for them as if they were my own. I love them all so dearly and wish nothing but the best for them. To start seeing my sister smile and be free from her chains of trauma makes me so proud to be called her sister. She too is a survivor.

This is the part of being a survivor that is sweet. You've had to face the most heart-breaking situations possible — but you can't let that destroy you. It may have broken you, and you've had to glue those pieces of your heart back together — but it hasn't entirely killed your soul. You've fought the good fight, and that is something to be immensely proud of.

And to you, reader — I won't ever know the real reason why you chose to read my book (unless you tell me), but all I can say is this: however my story has hit home for you, or if you're in a phase where you're just starting to learn about the term *narcissistic abuse* — I celebrate you for choosing my story to connect with. If you're someone on a painful journey, starting to connect the dots of your own trauma, then I feel for you. But just know — I was able to get out of it and make it to the other side. And you can too. You are not alone.

I now want to speak about a few key things that helped me on my journey of healing and surviving narcissistic abuse.

Independance

The reason I say independence is because you need to train your mind and heart not to rely on anyone. You need to start thinking for yourself and using your own internal voice to guide you. You need to be independent from the expectations and opinions of others. The many times I craved my parents' support and guidance and never received it meant I was often left to self-soothe my feelings or deal with my problems alone. No matter how many friends or even other family members you have to support you, if you pick up the phone every single time you need help, you'll never learn how to rely on yourself. Even though my sister was by my side, there have been plenty of battles I've had to fight alone. And even when you're rebuilding your life after trauma, there are times when you'll have to do it on your own. I've faced that many times. You might read this and fear the idea of being alone, but I'm telling you, it's not as scary as it sounds. To be able to stand on your own two feet is a skill that not many people possess. It puts your self-love on an incredibly high pedestal because instead of proving to others that you can do it, you've shown *yourself* that you can do it. That type of validation can't be sought from anyone else. This independence also gives you a radar to spot other narcissistic people you might come across because you've trained yourself to become so strong-minded, you won't believe people the minute you meet them. You'll have your guard up. You'll ask questions that many others won't. You'll be truth-seeking, trying to see if this person really is who they say they are. And remember, you can do all of this with a smile on your face. No need to let people know this is what you're doing, as many won't understand the life you've had to live.

Financial awareness

From my personal experience, I knew that I couldn't rely on my parents to support me financially, as they would either take my own money from me or throw it at my feet, as if I were unworthy of deserving it. That feeling of being worthless — of being a nobody in your own family home — pushed me to get a job from a young age, earn my own money, and keep my own money. That feeling was more satisfying, knowing that I earned that money through hard work, and it was mine to use as I wished. The awareness I had around money was that every individual has to earn a living, and unfortunately, no one is going to pay your bills or buy you nice things. That needs to come from yourself. I never went on shopping trips with my mum for her to treat me to anything. I never saw my dad willingly get his wallet out and give me money just because he loved me and wanted to see me happy. I began using my savings account from a young age because I knew the situation at home was so unstable — with being kicked out and with my mum crying over her own bills (even though, as I've mentioned, this was a victim-playing tactic). But when I was younger, I didn't see that. So instead, I began saving little by little for the day I could move out and not be chained to that house. A bit of foresight can confirm that those savings I had in my early 20s actually helped me move into my rented property and buy what I needed to live safely and comfortably. It might sound boring to some — when I could've gone on holidays and bought designer handbags if I wanted — but that fear was ingrained in me so strongly. The fear that at any minute, I could be out on the streets. Seeing my sister and brother already set up with their partners meant I had no choice but to think of a safety net for myself. To lastly add, even if you do have a partner you can rely on, I'd still make sure you've got some financial independence of your own. Because your partner can never replace the role of a generous parent. Good things do take time, and one day, financially, I won't have the same worries I did when I was younger.

Privacy

When dealing with narc parents, they will overstep your boundaries and invade any privacy that you have. They are so powerful that they'll even want to control your thoughts and play with your emotions. They sickly get a kick out of seeing a reaction from you. I learnt to start not telling my parents anything — even if I was, deep down, desperate to have a normal conversation with them, I knew this could never happen. I'd conceal anything important going on in my life — the result of my degree, promotions at work, getting a pay rise, my plans to move out eventually, who I was dating. Everything became a secret. You can't share your truth with an abusive parent because if it's good news, their jealousy won't allow them to be happy for you. And if it's bad news, they'll corner you, making you feel guilty for a downfall that wasn't even your fault.

I'd make sure my room was as clean and basic as possible to stop my mum from snooping, which was something she did often when I was a teenager, just to find anything she could to have a go at me for. Anything personal, or anything I wanted to hide, I would sometimes even store in my car. When arguing with a narc parent — and this is an extremely hard one — show as little emotion as possible. Be private with your actual emotions, because a narc parent will drain you of all your feelings and energy. They get a thrill out of it. The fact that you're not reacting and not crying, not shouting, and not screaming back will kill them. Because that's the reason for all their arguments: to get a reaction out of you. Keep those thoughts private too. Don't give anything away. If you're meeting up with other family members or people the narc wants control over, you'll need to hide this as well — say you're going to work, off to study, or meeting some other friends. As much as I am an honest person, I had to lie — only to them — in those situations, for the benefit of my own sanity. I'd say being private with your emotions is a skill — and it's a mastery that not many of us achieve in this lifetime, because we're only human. But try your best to be as disciplined as possible.

Acceptance

This is integral to your journey, healing, and moving forward. Radical acceptance is what it is called. This means that you need to truly accept that you are dealing — or have dealt — with a narcissist. This acceptance means you cannot change them. Don't even try to reason with them or hope that they will change their ways. These are people who have this personality because they chose to be this way. This isn't a medical condition. This isn't someone who needs fixing or needs help. When I began to accept my parents for who they truly are, this helped me a huge amount to not feel the confusion, the guilt, or even the shame for walking away and making the decisions I needed to make. You also have to accept that this person, no matter how they are connected to you, is first and foremost a narcissist. They aren't someone who has a *normal* side to them. Don't convince yourself you're getting roses when in fact you're being cut by thorns. You need to be confident enough to accept that you can make this move, this decision, on your own, and you do not need that narcissist in your life. What kind of person would decide to freely walk away from their parents? Who would want to give up their parents? Someone who simply didn't have another choice and knew that they were bringing your life down, rather than raising it up. The positive aspect is that the new life you can create for yourself doesn't involve a narcissist. And you don't need to earn this new life — you just need to accept to live it.

Knowledge

I'd lastly say that knowledge is power. This book may already be part of your knowledge journey, and you may have already learnt a lot of terms from the *narc guide* — but remember, reading one book isn't enough. There is so much factual information out there — through the internet, books, social media, and therapy — that can lead you to a place where you feel so empowered, you don't need to second-guess yourself. You will have tenfold of information to read and listen to about narc abuse that you won't know what to do with yourself. It seems to me the world's consciousness, as a collective, is coming together and calling out narcs — whether it's in the workplace, romantic relationships, family, places of worship, or even the government. A narc can be seen anywhere in plain sight, and that's why victims need to speak their truth. We are living in scary times. You will need to take steps like googling *Is my mum crazy?* or *Why is my dad so aggressive?* or *I don't feel loved at home.* Go with your feelings first, and then I promise, through research, the answers will come. I had so many mixed emotions for years trying to figure out what condition my mum had, because I was convinced she had one. Me and my sister just didn't realise it was narcissistic personality disorder. And before you even dream of getting the narc any help, stop. Don't. They will categorically not receive the help because they are so deluded. They believe nothing is wrong with them. I will list a few key resources below that helped me on my journey:

Dr Ramani Durvasula - This boss lady is everywhere, and I mean everywhere. One Google search and it will all come up: YouTube links, her books on Amazon, podcasts, and more. She paved the way for me and my sister.

www.daughtersofnarcissisticmothers.com - Danu Morrigan's website will give you a deep dive into narc abuse from the perspective of being a daughter, and it's specifically from your mother. Each narc acts differently with different people, which is why this type of abuse is so personal.

www.bepowerfulmedia.com - Of course, I need to include the community that helped me spread my wings with my truth and my story. Even though this isn't narc abuse specific, it shines a light on survivors from all types of traumatic backgrounds, including people who have suffered at the hands of a narc. The Powerful Books community offers so many insights and knowledge on how to overcome trauma, deal with external noise, and how to heal. I want to remind you that a parent can be causing you multiple types of abuse — not just narc abuse — so it's crucial to be well informed on *all* types of abuse. This group and page can help you navigate to the right resources for that.

I have been grateful for the process of achieving my dream of becoming an author. I honestly didn't think we would reach the dream in this way.

One reminder — only *you* can change your life. All the information and advice can be presented to you, but you need to find that core courage to initiate change.

Your new life will cost you your old one.

Linkin Park - Heavy is the crown

15

A NOTE TO THE SOUTH ASIAN COMMUNITY

South Asians, let's talk about it.

Now, there have been people — and will continue to be people — who judge me for my opinions towards the South Asian community. But that won't stop me from sharing my own views based on my own life experiences. I speak pretty openly about South Asian issues on social media, because I've found more of the younger generation are waking up to what it truly means to be *Indian*. This chapter is not about political or even racial issues in the community. This chapter is about the *man-made culture* we seem to accept, especially when it comes to what abuse looks like in Indian households.

I've discovered that South Asians will show blind loyalty to their family because they don't want the tradition of *shame* to be brought upon them. Even though it's become acceptable for all types of abuse to happen within the family, people suffer in silence because the image of the family is more important.

This is why abusers get away with their abuse. Instead of tackling these issues head-on, the culture wants to sweep it under the carpet — and they believe something as serious as parental abuse just goes away. Let me tell you, it never goes away. Not unless someone speaks up or something is done about it.

The culture is hell-bent on judging unmarried women in their 30s, but they fail to see that there are uncles and aunts enabling toxic behaviour within the family by making these judgements without knowing the full picture.

The culture believes that religion is the fix for every problem in life, and that it's up to *God* to decide the fate of the toxic family. But then my question is — if God is real, then why isn't he protecting the innocent in this lifetime? I avoid the religious Indians at all costs, because they don't want to take any responsibility. They'll throw it into the hands of God, when we know for a fact that God does nothing to change the situation.

South Asians will compete over who has the bigger house, the better car, and the child who's reached the highest educational status — but they forget that disability exists, that children can be part of the LGBTQ+ community, that bitter mother-in-laws get away with murder, and that some Indian men would rather worship their mothers than their wives. Indians put *Ma* on a pedestal — but a lot of these *mothers* are placed there without earning the right to be.

The South Asian culture needs to be held responsible for allowing domestic violence, sexual abuse, emotional abuse, and narcissistic abuse to stay hidden within the community, because this narrative doesn't help the victims; it helps the abusers. I could go on about how backwards the culture is in how we treat each other, but that would be another book. What I want to do instead is highlight how *different* I am from my own culture. But I'm still Indian — and I've done things *my way*. And doing things my way has benefited me in ways you could never imagine:

- Cut my abusive parents and toxic family out of my life.
- Spoke about my story on social media.
- Broke off an engagement.
- Lived independently as a single woman.
- Dated outside my race and ended up with a non-indian partner.
- Doesn't want to rush marriage.
- Can count her remaining family members on one hand.
- Encourages the younger Indian generations to live for themselves, not through the community or even their parents.
- Would rather have a dog than a child.
- Doesn't feel the need to 'cook' Indian food.
- Learns from other cultures and communities, and knows the importance of being open-minded.
- Isn't religious, and prefers spiritual practices instead.

Now, that above list will show any traditional South Asian person that I clearly don't align with being Indian, but the list below will show the parts of my culture that I *am* proud of. And I want to pave the way for women and men to be *Indian* in their own sense. There isn't one rulebook or one way to follow anything in life. Everything is individualistic and unique to your own journey.

- Can speak fluent Gujarati.
- Enjoys Indian music and the occasional movie.
- Enjoys Indian food.
- Appreciates the Indian fashion and jewellery industry.
- Applauds all the Indian women and men who are breaking societal norms and are the ones promoting peaceful protests to stop all forms of abuse.
- Doesn't believe women should shrink themselves to fit around the rest of the family.
- Doesn't believe that women are beneath men. We are equals.
- Doesn't believe I have to appease any family member out of forced practices.
- Loves the colour of my hair, eyes, and skin.
- Will always celebrate Diwali each year.

Now, there will be South Asian readers who still won't support my own life decisions on being Indian, but I think you all need to realise how quickly the world is evolving, and that it only takes one person to break the mould for others.

I am a strong, intelligent, beautiful Indian woman — and no one's opinion will take that away from me, whether you are brown or not.

The reason I wouldn't let anyone take this from me is because it took me a long journey to get to the place of accepting that I am from an Indian background. Growing up, there were many times I wanted to be seen as more of my *British* side rather than my heritage side. The main reason for this was that I didn't fit in with the family I was raised in. I felt like an outsider to my own family. I couldn't appreciate any of the culture back when I was a teenager, because I associated all Indian men with my abusive dad and complicit, judgemental brother, and all Indian women as my evil mum. They didn't teach me how to love my culture. Instead, they showed me that religion can be used to manipulate people, and that the culture is built on Bollywood. When I was away from home, I resonated more with Christianity, due to one of my best friends at the time coming from a devout Christian family. Even though we may have had different skin colour and features, I felt like we all had the same heart — and that's where I found peace and love. I went through an identity crisis between the ages of, I'd say, 15 to 18 — because I was truly unsure if I even wanted to be identified as Indian. All it felt like to me was that I was constantly battling with other Indian people, whether that be my own family or friends I'd made along the way. I feel, as humans, we all just want to belong somewhere, and I was trying to find my own place in the warped world that I lived in.

There was a moment where I wanted to convert to Christianity, because of the love, support, and community I had felt from joining my friend and her family on church days and events away. But that never happened, as I realised that changing my religion was not the answer to my prayers. The answers lay within myself. I needed to be a safe and secure person within myself before taking on the challenge of changing a core part of who I was. I needed to heal and love myself again, regardless of what religion I followed. Looking back, I'm so thankful I didn't go down that route of conversion. Even though it may work for some, I needed to find my own separate path. And I came to the conclusion that religion is not what helped me. What helped me was walking away from my abusive family and living a life of freedom — guided by the universe, and no religious or cultural entrapments of having to be a certain way to receive love.

16

SPIRITUAL CALLING

I want to share my devotion to being spiritual, because this has been the only thing that has shown me the light when all I ever knew was darkness. I can't pinpoint the exact moment I started my spiritual journey, but what I can tell you is that deep inside of me, I always knew there was more to this. More to this family system. More to this broken home.

I was determined to go and seek out those answers with the help of the universe. I would watch the seasons change, and myself stay the same. That small example of seasons changing made me think, *why can't things change for me? If every single year, every single day, I'm living in a changing world, why can't I change my world?* When I started questioning and not blindly following what was happening in my family, the universe was looking over and started throwing me signs. A lot of the time, those signs come from within. That voice inside your head — let it speak. Let it express. Let your intuition nudge you onto the path you need to be on. The funny thing about the universe, though, is that it won't always give you what you desire straight away. Unlike religion, where people pray for a better life or better possessions, the universe will always test you before you are delivered what you are destined to have. I've had countless times where I've begged the universe for my parents to change, or wished I were born into a completely different family. The universe would shake its head at me, because truthfully, that wasn't the hand I was dealt. My reality was different to many — but then again, who really lives a *normal* life? The universe began providing me with other things. Things in my life I hadn't even thought of. I had to lean into my spirituality through a lot of reading and spending plenty of time outside in nature. Because one thing they don't teach you about trauma is that nature is a natural healer. Nature doesn't judge, manipulate, or want a financial exchange from you. Nature just *lives*.

The trees and all their shades of green.

The sea and its rippling waves.

The birds that chirp every single morning.

The sun that rises and sets just the same.

The moon that offers solace on a dark night.

And the rain that provides water for growth.

All of these elements have played a crucial role in my life, and even now, I enjoy nothing more than being outside. Come rain or shine, being able to connect with nature, a blissfully innocent part of this world, makes me feel safe. It can even make me feel, at times, understood and heard. When it comes to humans, this isn't as easy — as I've learnt from the guidance of the universe that people can only meet you if they've met themselves. And I mean this in a soul context. Don't expect much from people — there's no guarantee they'll be who they say they are. Instead, focus on the vibrations and energy you feel from someone. That's your first instinct when meeting someone new. As time goes on, focus on that energy, and the more you protect your peace, the more the universe will connect you with the right people.

There have been times I've poured my heart out while sitting outside in nature — and it's unexplainable, but doing it that way is therapeutic for me. Spirituality is about energy exchange, and nature provides an abundance of energy. You may have seen it on social media, on the news, and read it in books, but I can't stress enough the importance of going for a walk and breathing in fresh air to clear your clogged-up mind. Picking up your phone and scrolling through social media — seeing humans being fake and wishing for a life you never had — only makes things worse. I've always wanted to connect with a cause deeply, and spirituality offers me that. It doesn't take much for me to go out and explore the world and see what it has to offer. Animals are another one of the world's greatest gifts. No matter how big or small, they don't need to speak — but they communicate in the most compassionate, honest way. A way in which humans never could. That's where my love for dogs especially comes from. The world has so much for you — you just need to know where to seek, and it will provide. There may be people who don't understand the concept of spirituality or find it *weird*, but let me tell you — if I'm living proof that I've conquered a lot of suffering because of spirituality, then it's not something to be mocked.

17

DID I EVER LIKE THEM?

When someone is in your life for a very long time, your mind can't help but form attachments, create memories, and store information about this person that may not even be relevant to you. I believe that you can't just forget about people — even if you've gone no contact and they may be "dead to you" — you can't truly forget how someone made you feel or what you observed of them.

For me, knowing my parents since birth meant that I acquired all this information about them, and some may ask, "Was there anything you liked about your parents?" I can't seem to answer that question because anything I picked up from them, like how my dad likes certain Indian music and how my mum used to use lipstick on her cheeks as a blusher, were just mere observations. This type of information is still stored in my head because I believe a child who goes through abuse will try to find any moments, no matter how small, to connect with the parent. So, me remembering that useless information was, at the time, almost a safety response. My brain was either constantly trying to survive, or it was trying to form a safe connection with my parents. Neither of which I truly succeeded in. I was always torn between trying to survive, make sense of my situation, and still trying to make my living environment livable. So I'd pick up on things my parents liked — to try and use as a connector if I needed to. In trauma, we have a response called *hypervigilance*, which means you are extremely sensitive to your environment, and your levels of alertness stay heightened as your nervous system is trying to regulate what's around you. This was the response I lived in for the majority of my life, and still, subconsciously, I can be in a state of hypervigilance. So on reflection, no, there's nothing I liked about my parents. In fact, most of the time now, I view them as failures. However, what's important to know is that because I was in a state of hypervigilance, I still hold those memories — the interests and the things they liked — because I was trying to connect with them on some level for my own safety. And deep down, that *wanting* of a parent was always there.

18

LIFE AFTER TRAUMA

The narrative of my story has been changed, altered, and destroyed so many times. Whether that be gossip from people, the evil side of social media, or even the ones closest to me doubting my experiences. One thing I can say is that this tangible book you are reading is the only true narrative of my life up until now. These pages have come straight from the heart, and this book is a testament to anyone who thought I may have just been "doing this all for attention". What those people fail to realise is — I don't need the attention of strangers. What my younger self really needed was the attention of her *parents*.

I walk through life as a different person now. I've evolved, changed, and adapted to many situations, but one thing that's stayed the same is my truth, the heart I have as a person, and my own moral code that I live by.

Unfortunately, people in general can be your biggest blessings in life — or your worst enemies. And half the time, we don't get to see who is who.

Always stay true to *you*. Don't let anyone else control your life.

Fiercely love the people who are good to you, and walk away from the ones who are bad for you.

Now that I am fully in control of my life, I've been able to live in bliss.

The feeling of this can't be explained to someone who hasn't experienced the type of abuse I have, because the majority of my years were spent in survival and escapism mode.

I wasn't allowed to express who I wanted to be. I was mocked and belittled for many of my life choices.

When I did make a life choice, the heavy feeling was always there that I had to share it with my parents. And I knew they'd be disapproving, spread the news to other family members without my consent, or simply not be interested at all. My parents only live by one rule: *only when it suits them*.

I feel as though I've claimed back a huge chunk of my life. There are days when I want to reclaim who I wanted to be at 10, at 17, at 21, at 25 — so I listen to my soul on days like this and give myself what I need. Because all of that was taken away from me.

Life after trauma now feels like warm summer days. It feels like a calm, bubbling lake. It sounds like laughter from a loved one. And it reminds me — every day — that I'm alive. There are still days when I feel triggered. Days when I feel deeply upset. But the majority of the time, I feel blissful.

Finally feeling like the main character in the story I call *my life*.

I don't know what my future holds, or where life will take me — but I know for certain it's better than the life I left behind.

19

FOR YOU

This chapter is for you. Feel free to write, journal, or make notes on the following pages. This is a safe space.

My story began when I entered this world — and pen touched paper when I was around 14 or 15 years old. I published my first book at 30.

You have a story inside you too.

So, when does your story start?

Is it now?

TELL YOUR TRUTH

TELL YOUR TRUTH

ABOUT THE AUTHOR

You can reach me on either channel below:

Instagram - sonam.story
Tiktok - sonams_story
Email - sonam.story@gmail.com

www.ingramcontent.com/pod-product-compliance
Lightning Source LLC
Chambersburg PA
CBHW070456100426
42743CB00010B/1642